Pretending to be Normal

of related interest

Asperger's Syndrome
A Guide for Parents and Professionals
Tony Attwood
ISBN 1 85302 577 1

Eating an Artichoke
A Mother's Perspective on Asperger's Syndrome
Echo Fling
ISBN 1 85302 711 1

Discovering My Autism
Apologia Pro Vita Sua (with Apologies to Cardinal Newman)
Edgar Schneider
ISBN 1 85302 724 3

Through the Eyes of Aliens
A Book about Autistic People
Jasmine Lee O'Neill
ISBN 1 85302 710 3

Autism: An Inside-Out Approach
An Innovative Look at the Mechanics of 'Autism'
and its Developmental 'Cousins'
Donna Williams
ISBN 1 85302 387 6

Children with Autism, Second Edition
Diagnosis and Interventions to Meet Their Needs
Colwyn Trevarthen, Kenneth Aitken, Despina Papoudi and Jacqueline Robarts
ISBN 1 853 02 555 0

The ADHD Handbook
A Guide for Parents and Professionals
Alison Munden and Jon Arcelus
ISBN 1 85302 756 1

From Thoughts to Obsessions
Obsessive Compulsive Disorder in Children and Adolescents
Per Hove Thomsen
ISBN 1 85302 721 9

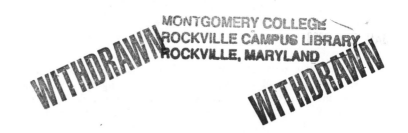
Pretending to be Normal
Living with Asperger's Syndrome

Liane Holliday Willey

Foreword by Tony Attwood

Jessica Kingsley Publishers
London and Philadelphia

First published in the United Kingdom in 1999 by
Jessica Kingsley Publishers Ltd,
116 Pentonville Road,
London N1 9JB, England
and
325 Chestnut Street,
Philadelphia, PA 19106, USA.

www.jkp.com

Copyright © 1999 Liane Holliday Willey
Foreword copyright © 1999 Tony Attwood

Second impression 2000

Library of Congress Cataloging in Publication Data
A CIP catalog record for this book is available from the Library of Congress

British Library Cataloguing in Publication Data
Willey, Liane Holliday
Pretending to be normal : living with Asperger's syndrome
1.Willey, Liane Holliday 2.Asperger's syndrome – Patients – Biography
3.Asperger's syndrome – Popular works
I.Title
362.1'968982'0092

ISBN 1 85302 749 9

Printed and Bound in Great Britain by
Athenaeum Press, Gateshead, Tyne and Wear

Contents

DEDICATION 7

FOREWORD 9

ACKNOWLEDGMENTS 11

AUTHOR'S NOTE 12

INTRODUCTION 13

Remembering When 17

The Gap Widens and Wondering Why 31

Losing My Way 47

A Slow Walk Home 63

Crossing the Bridge 77

Rocking My Babies 93

Settling In, But Never Down 107

Appendices

I. Explaining Who You Are to Those Who Care 123

II. Survival Skills for AS College Students 131

III. Employment Options and Responsibilities 141

IV. Organizing Your Home Life 149

V. Coping Strategies for Sensory Integration Dysfunction 155

VI. Thoughts for Non-AS Support People 161

VII. Support Groups and Other Helpful Resources 167

GLOSSARY 171

REFERENCES 175

Foreword

Liane's autobiography will allow others to understand the world as perceived by a person with Asperger's Syndrome. As a consequence of this condition she is a bewildered stranger in our social world. She eloquently describes herself as one of those *'people who never quite find their way, but never quite lose it either'*. She has a daughter with Asperger's Syndrome and her child's diagnosis led to her recognition that she shares the same condition. Liane currently teaches her daughter the strategies that have helped her to navigate her way through, to use her term, the *regular* world. The value of writing about her lifelong journey of exploration is that those with Asperger's Syndrome will recognise the same perceptions, thoughts and experiences. She is a fellow traveller. She offers genuine hope for the future in that she has eventually succeeded in finding a partner who understands and supports her. She also has success in her career, and considers that *'most of my Asperger's Syndrome traits continue to fade away'*.

Families and friends of people with Asperger's Syndrome will achieve a new perspective on a child or adult who may not have been able to coherently explain their point of view. Liane is their advocate and parents will turn every page of her autobiography, eager to know what happened next and how she coped, so that they can apply their new understanding to their son or daughter. I strongly recommend this book for teachers as it will provide the previously elusive reasons for behaviours that were considered unconventional or appeared to be abnormal. Specialists and therapists who diagnose and treat such children will find the book a treasure trove of information and insight. I will be using many of Liane's quotations to explain the nature of the syndrome and employ her strategies to help the individuals that I support. It is interesting that at the end of the book, Liane states that '...*no matter the hardships, I do not wish for a cure to Asperger's Syndrome. What I wish for is a cure for the common ill that pervades too many lives; the ill that makes people compare themselves to a normal that is measured in terms of perfect and absolute standards, most of which are impossible for anyone to reach.'* This has profound cultural and philosophical implications for everyone.

When Liane sent me her manuscript, she attached a note that read: *'Hope you like the book. Your friend, Liane.'* Not only am I honoured to be considered her friend, I also consider her a hero whose book will be an inspiration for thousands of people throughout the world.

Dr Tony Attwood, February 1999

Acknowledgments

So many people have touched my life with goodness, most times without realizing it. If it were not for their support, I would still be pretending. My most heartfelt thanks to...

- Tony Attwood for his dedication to everyone in the Asperger community.
- All the AS friends I met through the OASIS web site who taught me so much of what I now know.
- Sarah Abraham and Lisa Dyer for their never ending guidance and support.
- The Reverend Richard Curry for showing me how to catch the spirit.
- My favorite friend Oliver Weber for his laughter and his bear hugs.
- Maureen Willey for being my sister.
- Margo Smith for being my friend.
- My mother Janett Holliday for giving me tenacity, fortitude and courage.
- My father John T Holliday, Jr for teaching me how to think independently, virtuously and honorably.
- My husband Thomas Willey, for holding my hand no matter what I do.
- My precious and perfect daughters, Lindsey, Jenna and Meredith, for giving me the strength that renews me, the joy that lifts my soul, and the love that lets my heart know it will never have to pretend again.

And finally, my deepest gratitude to the God in heaven who answered when I called.

Author's Note

Tony Attwood, in his book *Asperger's Syndrome: A Guide for Parents and Professionals* (1998), offers the point that many adults find they have AS only after a relative's diagnosis brings it to their attention. So it was in our case. My seven-year-old daughter received an AS label one year ago. Her diagnosis opened the door to self-awareness for my family and me. We had never heard of AS, but once we did, we began to see its traits and characteristics in many family members, myself included.

I have never been evaluated for AS. To date, I have not been able to find anyone in my geographic area who evaluates AS in adults. But that is okay. I do not really need a formal diagnosis to tell me what I already know. What I do need is more information about how to help my daughter, more information about how to continue my own growth, more information about how to help the public understand AS. It is my hope that those who read this book will begin their own road to discovery, either for themselves or for someone they care about.

Liane Holliday Willey

Introduction

The autism umbrella is vast. Within its boundaries is a wide range of abilities and disabilities; a wide range of differences. It is a fluid diagnosis, one that has no definite beginning and no certain end. Scientists are uncertain as to how it is caused. Educators debate how to manage it. Psychologists are baffled about how to differentiate among its various labels. Parents are not certain how to deal with any of it. And those with autism are too often without any voice at all. Autism touches many, and yet, it is one of the most misunderstood developmental disorders.

This book peers under the umbrella of autism and looks at Asperger's Syndrome (AS), a relatively new autism-related diagnosis, first discussed by Hans Asperger in 1944, but generally unheard of until researchers, including Uta Frith, Lorna Wing and Tony Attwood, brought it to international attention in the 1990s. People with AS, like their autistic cousins, have impairments in socialization, communication and imagination, albeit to a less significant degree. According to the diagnostic criteria set forth by Gillberg and Gillberg (1989), people with AS have: social interaction impairments, narrow interests, an insistence on repetitive routines, speech and language peculiarities, non-verbal communication problems and motor clumsiness. That having been said, it is essential to realize that each of these symptoms is manifested in a variety of unique and diverse ways, depending upon the overall abilities of the person affected. Within AS, there is a wide range of function. In truth, many AS people will never receive a diagnosis. They will continue to live with other labels or no label at all. At their best, they will be the eccentrics who wow us with their unusual habits and stream-of-conscious creativity, the inventors who give us wonderfully unique gadgets that whiz and whirl and make our life surprisingly more manageable, the geniuses who discover new mathematical equations, the great musicians and writers and artists who enliven our lives. At their most neutral, they will be the loners who never know quite how to greet us, the aloof who aren't sure they want to greet us, the collectors who know everyone at the flea market by name and birth date, the non-conformists who cover their cars in bumper stickers, a few of the professors everyone has in college. At their most noticeable, they will be the lost souls who invade our personal space, the regulars at every diner who carry on complete conversations with the group ten tables away, the people who sound suspiciously like robots, the characters who insist they wear the same socks and eat the same breakfast day in and day out, the people who never quite find their way but never quite lose it either.

The prognosis for those with AS is quite variable. Much depends not only on the person's ability, but also on the match between the intervention programs and the needs of the AS individual, the support system of everyone involved and the continued committed influence of the medical and educational communities. Yet, prognosis is a very relative term, and as such, I would never attempt to quantify who has a better quality of life based upon their degree of AS. By that I mean, if we are only interested in changing the AS person so that they can better meld themselves into society – a tenuous and nebulous concept to begin with – then perhaps we are misguided. The AS community gives us much cause to celebrate. Never, I think, should we expect or want them to be carbon copies of the most socially adept among us. We should only suggest whatever help they need to insure they have every opportunity of leading productive, rewarding and self-sufficient lives. We would lose too much and they would lose even more, if our goal were anything more, or less.

Perhaps Tony Attwood (1998) captures this thought best when he says of AS individuals '...they are a bright thread in the rich tapestry of life. Our civilization would be extremely dull and sterile if we did not have and treasure people with Asperger's Syndrome' (pp.184–185). ·

1

Remembering When

There are days when I stand on a precipice, precariously ready to fall beyond whom I am and into someone whom I cannot really believe I ever was; someone I beg never to become again. These are my worst epochs. They are dark and rude and shocking and dangerous. They compel me to issue surrender, to pervade the abyss. There are days when I stand on a terrace, ready and able to embrace new insight and a clean awareness. These are the days that make me whole, for they led me to the understanding that looking back does not mean I will go backward. Remembering can teach me who I am and guide me toward who I will be. Remembering can set me free. Most often I settle on a great divide, carefully balancing my past with my today. I like it that way. I like being able to revisit my past, but only when I bring along a measure of clinical behaviorism. I would never turn back in search of regrets or mistakes or misdirected thoughts. I simply use my past as a catalyst for conscious thought and for self-appreciation. Though it has taken thirty eight years, I cannot express what a relief I feel to finally 'get' me!

I remember a man handing me a big fat black crayon. I knew he expected me to use the crayon as a pencil. I wondered why he didn't just give me a pencil. The crayon was ugly. It was flat. It should have been round. It was almost too big to hold. I didn't like the way it smoothed itself all over the vanilla paper, it was too slick and messy. But I used it anyway. My mother had prepared me for the visit. She told me I was going to take a test that would tell us how smart I was. She told me not to be nervous and she promised me ice cream when the test was finished. If it weren't for the ice cream, I don't think I would have held that nasty crayon. But I did. I drew little pictures and circled sentences and built things with blocks. I knew I was smart and I knew the test was dumb.

By the time I was three years old, my parents knew I was not an average child. My pediatrician suggested they have me evaluated by a psychiatrist. Several conversations and an IQ test later, my diagnosis was decided: gifted and indulged. Smart and spoiled. With that knowledge in tow, my parents began to evaluate their only child according to a new set of blueprints. From that moment on, everything I did was simply and efficiently explained with a nod, a wink and a 'well, she is a bit spoiled' musing. Little did they know.

When I think of my earliest years, I recall an overwhelming desire to be away from my peers. I much preferred the company of my imaginary friends. Penny and her brother Johnna were my best friends, though no one saw them but me. My mother tells me I used to insist that we set them a place at the table, include them on our car trips, and treat them like they were real beings. I remember going into my mom's room with nothing more than boxes of tin foil and Penny and Johnna. Together we would make elaborate table settings out of the tin foil. Plates, cups, silverware, serving platters, even food. I don't remember playing tea party, only that I made the things a tea party would need.

I also remember playing school with my pretend friends. Each year, after our real elementary school closed for the summer, I would climb in the dumpsters behind the classrooms and dig through the reams of trash to collect old textbooks and mimeographs and workbooks. I wanted real school supplies; pretend items didn't work in this case. I would take all my finds home and treat them with great respect. I loved those treasures. I can still feel what it was like to open the books so wide their covers touched back to back. I remember the way the book would resist my forcing it to open that far-reaching. I remember feeling annoyed that it would not lend itself more willingly. I liked running my finger down the little valley the book formed at its center when it was opened as far as it could go. It was smooth and straight and calming. I also liked to bury my nose in its middle and smell the familiar scent that clings to books stored among chalk and erasers and paint, and then held by children. If I found this smell wasn't present, I lost interest in that book and turned to one that did. My favorite find was the old purple ditto worksheets schools used before more sophisticated copy machines came along. I still smell the ink of fresh dittos. I love that smell. The dittos were nice to stack, especially when I had a lot of them. I liked the sound and the feel that came from lightly dropping them up and down between my hands until they met the hard surface I used to help me render them straight.

Using the materials to teach Penny and Johnna was of secondary importance. Far more interesting to me was the arranging of the supplies. Like with my tea parties, the fun came from setting up and arranging things. Maybe this desire to organize things rather than play with things is the reason I never had a great interest in my peers. They always wanted to use the things I had so carefully arranged. They would want to rearrange and redo. They did not let me control the environment. They did not act the way I thought they should act. Children needed more freedom than I could provide them.

I don't believe I ever felt compelled to share any of my toys, my ideas or anything else that was mine. If I did decide to play with a friend other than my imaginary ones, it was typically with a little girl named Maureen (who is still my best friend). Even now, Maureen teases me with stories that involve her scheming to hide her other playmates when I came to visit her at her home. It seems I became very hostile if I were to discover she had betrayed me by inviting someone else to play. For my part, I vividly remember hating to see her with anyone other than me. I don't believe I was jealous. I know it wasn't simple insecurities. I didn't give other children enough thought to warrant those emotions. I simply could not see the point in having more than one friend and I could never imagine Maureen might feel any differently. To me, the logic was simple. I had my friend. She had me. End of story. Anyone else was an obvious intrusion, an intrusion that, if allowed, would force me into a very uncomfortable and generally impossible situation. If another little child were allowed in our circle, I would then be expected to play with that child, too.

I never understood group dynamics, particularly casual friendship dynamics that work on giving and taking, role playing and modeling, rule following and turn taking. Somewhere along the way, I had learned to cope with the intricacies of young friendships well enough to manage one friend. Any more spelled disaster sometimes in very real forms. One day, I suppose I had had enough of Maureen's having other friends. She and a little girl from next door were playing outside in the yard when I marched myself up to the little girl and asked her just why she was at Maureen's house. I can't remember what she told me, but I do remember I punched her right in the belly the moment she finished her explanation. I guess she said something I didn't like!

My mother enrolled me in a ballet class when I was six years old to help me with my inability to enjoy my peers. While this seemed a good plan, it was very short lived. To begin with, I disliked ballet in general. I could not for the life of me master the intricateness of it all; the coordination of bilateral movement it requires. My mind was simply unable to prepare a way for my body to understand first position or second position or any position that meant one leg had to go one way and the other another while my arms went still a different direction. Ballet frustrated and confused me. What did it mean to move like a swan? Would a swan wear leotards that strangled or slippers that made your toes go to sleep? Ballet and my teacher made no sense. At least none I could fathom. The children made no sense either. They refused to follow the rules. Sooner than later, ballet had worn out its welcome with me, and I with it. I often wonder if my teacher was delighted or dismayed to make the call that led to my never returning to class.

'Mrs. Holliday, we think it would be in everyone's best interest if Liane no longer attended our school,' the teacher began.

'Why would you suggest that?' my mother responded.

'To begin with, she is quite uncoordinated. But her worst offence is her attitude. Not only is she uncooperative, she also refuses to get along with others. In fact, she hits the poor children whose only failing is standing near her.'

When my mother asked me why I hit the poor children in my class, I gave an answer that to me, was self-explanatory.

'Because they touched me.'

'What do you mean 'because they touched you'?' Mom asked.

'We're supposed to stay an arm away from each other. We are not supposed to touch.'

'But Liane, they don't mean to touch you. They probably just lose their balance and accidentally run into you.'

'They aren't supposed to touch me,' was the only reply I would give. Made sense to me. And so ended my ballet career.

Words were beginning to mean far more to me than actions were. I remember following directions, literally and to the letter. As was her habit, Mom insisted I be able to see the roof of my house from wherever I was. This was her way of insuring I never wandered off too far. One afternoon, I remember making my way to my elementary school playground, never fearing that four blocks was too far away. After all, I told my mother when I returned home and found her terribly upset, I had been able to see the roof of my home. So what if I had had to climb to the roof of my school to do so. That's how I understood language. Words had yet to develop into metaphors or similes or analogies or main ideas. It was all about details and pedantic rules and one-way semantics. I never considered a statement had more than one meaning. I always assumed the meaning I inferred was the intent of the speaker. Today, we know we need to help children with AS learn that other people have other points of views. Back when I was young, we simply assumed children were innately equipped with this knowledge. My parents, assuming I was acting audaciously, were constantly baffled as to why I found it so necessary to challenge their authority. They found themselves weighing their every directive to be certain I would not find a way to weave their words with mine. Which is of course, exactly what I did. I had to make their language fit into mine. I was not able to make mine fit into theirs.

Typically, my teachers took it upon themselves to analyze this pedantic behavior of mine and I'm told their fondest memories of me included adjectives like obstinate, disobedient and everyone's favorite, mentally retarded. Because my parents were learning how to talk to me, it never occurred to them that I was not following other people's directions. They knew how to get my attention, usually by allowing me the freedom to find my own way of expressing my interests. If I wanted to chew the same piece of gum for days on end, that was fine. If I wanted to shape my mouth into the letters they were forming while I spoke, that was okay. If I insisted on reading my books out loud that was okay too, even if we were in the library. They knew I had my own way of doing things, and they didn't interfere with my methods so long as the effort was genuine and the result positive. I had control over my learning environment at home and because I was so academically gifted, my parents saw no reason to interfere with a good thing. But at school, the rules changed. Suddenly, I was expected to comply with agendas and schedules that were stifling and illogical.

During my first year of school, the teacher assigned each of us a special number. This number was supposed to be our special number and every time she called our number we were to answer, as if she had called us by name. To my way of thinking, this was a meaningless idea. Naturally, I refused to comply. The teacher called my parents and told them as much. My parents agreed with me that this was a silly issue and they insisted the teacher use my name from then on out.

That same year, we were required to take naps each day. I vividly remember my teacher announcing, 'Children, find your mats and take your nap.' I refused. Again, the teacher called my parents. Again, my parents made their way to the school.

'Liane, why won't you take your nap?' my parents wondered of me.

'Because, I can't.'

'You see!' the teacher said smugly.

'Why can't you take your nap?' my parents continued.

'Because I don't have a mat.'

'You most certainly do have a mat. There it is in your cubby,' the teacher replied.

'I do not have a mat.'

'You see what I mean?' the teacher asked my parents. 'She is an obstinate child.'

'Why do you say you don't have a mat?' the folks asked, not giving up on me.

'That is not a mat. That is a rug,' I honestly and accurately replied.

'So it is,' said my father. 'Will you take a nap on your rug?'

'If she tells me to,' I said matter-of-factly.

'Tell her to take her nap on her rug,' my father said as my parents turned to take me home. I think even then, I was grateful to be vindicated. I wasn't trying to be difficult, I was trying to do the right thing. The trouble was, the teacher assumed I understood language like other children did. I did not.

Most children thrive on chaos and noise. Children in school were always running and shouting and moving. They were always busy, always mixing things up, never content to play quietly or by themselves. I liked to play at the kitchen center in our kindergarten room. In fact, I rarely wanted to play anywhere else, another 'problem' of mine that caused my teacher great distress. If I wasn't playing with the kitchen toys, I was reading. Reading was relaxing and it was something I could do very well by the time I was three years old. Should I say, it looked like I could read. Actually, I could call out most of the words printed in my books. I could not typically comprehend the material if it was written above a first grade level. Nonetheless, I did find solace in the dark print so neatly typed on the white pages. I enjoyed the rhythmic pattern and the flow that moved the eye from left to right, from top to bottom. I welcomed the routine that insisted I stop for periods and break for commas and new paragraphs. I loved the way most words played on my tongue. I loved the way they caused different parts of my mouth to move. But if I did come across a word that hurt my ears, typically words with too many hyper-nasal sounds, I would not say them aloud. Similarly, I would refuse words that looked ugly by virtue of being too lopsided or too cumbersome or too unusual in their phonetics. I don't recall being very attracted to picture books, probably because these required I attach meaning to what I saw. Word books did not require this of me. Word books allowed me to take what I needed and then move on.

By around eight years old, I had become a very proficient comprehender as well as word caller. So long as the material was of a factual nature. Fiction was more difficult for me for it forced my thoughts to go beyond the literal. I preferred biographies and eventually made my way through every biography we had in our library, despite the librarian's repeated request that I check out something new and different. I liked reading about real live people and their real life experiences. It didn't matter if it was a story about Babe Ruth or Harry Truman or Harriet Tubman. I wasn't attracted to baseball or government or social issues so much as I was attracted to the reality of the words I was reading. Even today, as I find those same biographies on the shelves of libraries, I return to that old comfortable place in my mind where those words meant so much to me.

Unlike most children, I hated active outings, particularly outings to new places, so completely that I used to become physically ill just thinking about making the visit. My mother remembers dreading birthday parties and trips to amusement parks and parades and visits to grandma's house, principally because I was certain to throw up just as we were on our way to the event. We can laugh about this now, but we both know it was anything but funny at the time. Neither of us understood why I seemed to find life so difficult. Every child wanted to go to birthday parties or to visit grandma. Every child, so it seemed, but me. Sleep overs too, were impossible for me, even though I tried and tried to actually make one work. They never did and each time my father would come to get me and take me home.

I hated leaving my home. It made sense to me. I knew where my books were. I could depend on my dog to follow my orders. I could run my fingers along the ridges our yellow plates made as they stood in their neat stacks in our square pantry. I could stuff things down our laundry shoot, over and over again. I could slide up and down our hardwood hall. I could line up my stuffed animals and talk to them without having to bother with needless interruptions. I could hide under my bed if I needed to.

Many a time, my actions brought my parents and me to the hospital. I loved to chew crunchy things, even if they were poisonous. When I was finished with my little tin foil table settings, I used to chew them until they crackled their way into a tight, neat ball. I shaved the sand from Emory boards with my front teeth. I took great delight in grinding the striking strip of a match book between my back teeth. I chewed sugar packets whole, loving the way the grainy sweet sugar overcame the bitter paper packet. I ate school paste and play dough and paraffin. I might have avoided the trips to the hospital if I had stopped my grazing there. Unfortunately, I also enjoyed toilet bowl sanitizing bars and moth balls. My parents tell me people at the hospital began to suspect them of child abuse. I suspect they must have grown accustomed to my idiosyncracies.

As much as I loved to chew scratchy and gritty textures, I often found it impossible even to touch some objects. I hated stiff things, satiny things, scratchy things, things that fit me too tightly. Thinking about them, imagining them, visualizing them... any time my thoughts found them, goose bumps and chills and a general sense of unease would follow. I routinely stripped off everything I had on even if we were in a public place. I constantly threw my shoes away, often as we were driving in the car. I guess I thought that would get rid of the nasty things forever! I ripped the tags right out of my clothing even though I knew I would get in trouble for the hole that was left in the tag's place. I think I was almost five years old before I was persuaded to wear anything other than my favorite pair of blue nubby polyester shorts.

I also found many noises and bright lights nearly impossible to bear. High frequencies and brassy, tin sounds clawed my nerves. Whistles, party noisemakers, flutes and trumpets and any close relative of those sounds disarmed my calm and made my world very uninviting. Bright lights, mid-day sun, reflected lights, strobe lights, flickering lights, fluorescent lights; each seemed to sear my eyes. Together, the sharp sounds and the bright lights were more than enough to overload my senses. My head would feel tight, my stomach would churn, and my pulse would run my heart ragged until I found a safety zone.

I found solace underwater. I loved the sensation that came from floating with the water. I was liquid, tranquil, smooth; I was hushed. The water was solid and strong. It held me safe in its black, awesome darkness and it offered me quiet – pure and effortless quiet. Entire mornings would pass me by while I swam underwater for great periods of time, pushing my lungs to hold on to the quiet and the dark until they forced me to find air.

Though my pool was my favorite safety zone, I had others. I often found comfort among the strong arms of a great maple tree we had in our back yard. In the tree, I could watch everything around me without having to interact. I could take part in the world as an observer. I was an avid observer. I was enthralled with the nuances of people's actions. In fact, I often found it desirable to become the other person. Not that I consciously set out to do that, rather it came as something I simply did. As if I had no choice in the matter. My mother tells me I was very good at capturing the essence and persona of people. At times, I literally copied someone's look and their actions. For instance, if a schoolmate began wearing glasses, I would sneak my aunt's so that I too could wear glasses, even though they nearly blinded me. If someone broke their arm, I would come home and complain my own arm was broken, until my mother finally cast it in flour paste.

But often, I would engage in far more assimilating behaviors. I was uncanny in my ability to copy accents, vocal inflections, facial expressions, hand movements, gaits, and tiny gestures. It was as if I became the person I was emulating. I don't know how I choose who to copy, but I do know they were always someone I found pretty, though not necessarily pretty in the usual sense. I don't think I paid much attention to the overall appearance of the person. I remember being attracted to pieces of people's faces. I might have liked the color of the eyes, the texture of the hair or the straightness of the teeth. But it was the nose that really held my interest. Straight, linear, 'classic' noses appealed to my sense of balance. Button noses, turned-up noses, crooked noses, and especially short and smooshy noses, sent me staring in dismay. I wanted to rush to their face and remold their nose. I would give no thought to the bones and the cartilage that lie just beneath the surface of the nose. To me, the form was pliable and stretchable. And because of those thoughts, I found no reason why anyone's nose should deviate from the linear.

My parents tell me they were often confused not so much by my ability to copy others, but rather by my desire to do so. They thought I was giving in to peer pressure or wanting to be someone I was not. This was not the case during that time in my life. Until I was somewhere around ten years old, I held myself separate from others. I never really compared who I was to who they were. It didn't dawn on me to see myself as a fellow third grader or as a member of a team. I felt almost like I was invisible. I was conscious of the fact that other people could see me and hear me and talk to me, but still I thought I was removed from their domain. I didn't contemplate that they ostracized me; rather, I chose to shut them out. I could stare at them all I liked, never thinking this might annoy them. I could take in parts of who they were and never worry that I was a copy cat, never worry I had lost me. I always knew right where I was.

If I did begin to lose me, I knew how to get me back. Under my bed, I had a wonderfully symmetrical alcove made from the form of my headboard. The alcove was no more than three feet wide by two feet deep, and in it I could always find myself. Whenever things became too fuzzy or too loud or too distracting; whenever I began to feel as though I would come unraveled, I knew I could crawl into my alcove and crunch up into it until I felt as square and symmetrical as it. I could squeeze my knees and pull my thoughts back into my bones so they could end their flight through my blood and rest for awhile. I could plug my ears shut with my index fingers and grit my teeth and clamp my eyes closed and drift about in the stillness of it all. Then, when I was ready, I would open my eyes and there I would be, all safe and sound.

By the time I was approaching my second year in school, I had developed several public appearance coping strategies. Unlike some children who find success through a well crafted offensive, I preferred to retreat and rely on a quiet defence. If things grew too uncomfortable or confusing for me, I simply drew back and seethed. I'm certain there was nothing charming about my behavior, but I do know it brought a more positive connotation than raging did. Not that I didn't have temper tantrums. I did, and apparently quite often if my babysitting aunts tell the truth. According to them, I could turn on a dime from being a calm, collected and rather quiet child, to one that seemed filled with the energy of a roaring tornado. One moment would find me calmly working on a project – typically building houses and towns out of paper or cardboard boxes – and the next I would be stomping the hard work into piles of scraps. My aunts were never certain why I flew into a rage; I never told them my reasons. I suspect I flipped the moment my sensory system became overloaded. I don't think I knew how to diffuse myself when I was caught between something I really wanted to do and the problem that came from my sensory integration dysfunction. I imagine I just held on as long as I could and then, unable to realize when enough was enough, I let loose with rage and tantrums.

I'm not certain why I never allowed myself to tantrum in public, but I do have an inkling of an idea that might offer an explanation. I remember watching other children as they threw fits. It was horrible to watch them, to see their little bodies twist into odd contortions and their face turn red and sometimes purple, just as their lips made their way to blue. They were no longer children. Right before my eyes, they became molten, hot and savage. Maybe my horrified association with that behavior became a catalyst for self-control. Maybe I just knew that so long as I kept my rage at home, I would not be in jeopardy of becoming that misshapen creature from the grocery store.

I realize my early childhood might sound cheerless, even strangely foreign, but it wasn't. Not to me. Images came to me like motion pictures on the screen and I enjoyed the sensation that came from thinking life was something set forth for me to enjoy at my leisure. I could jump in when I felt like it, slip away if that fit, or sit back and observe as a wandering passerby would. It never dawned on me that other children were reasoning with the world far differently than I was. It never dawned on my parents either. I think my peers knew I was different, but they were far too young and unsophisticated to care much either way. I knew how to find safety and warmth when I was a little girl. I often wished, as I grew older, to return to that time and place. I often wish that now.

Looking back, I can easily see why my parents, my psychiatrist and my pediatrician dismissed my actions as precocious or creative alternatives to the norm. Thoughts of anything related to autism would have been the farthest thing from their consciousness. Children with autism lived in a world of their own. They often hurt themselves, shrieked, raged and never spoke. They were institutionalized, with no hope for a better tomorrow. So everyone believed. Thoughts of a simple learning disability would also have been far from their thoughts. I was gifted. Gifted children did not have learning disabilities forty years ago. So too did they believe.

Now that my parents understand AS, they are able to describe my childhood with the help of an entirely new perspective; one that makes the choices I made then, as well as the choices I make as an adult, seem far more focused and clear, perhaps even more correct, given the way I perceive the world. Today, when we discuss yesterday, there are many 'ah ha' experiences. Lots of 'So that's why...' discussions. Some 'We just assumed...' conversations. There is no guilt, no blaming, no wondering about 'what ifs'. Today, there is harmony. There is order. There is cohesiveness.

2

The Gap Widens
and Wondering Why

My reflection is clear in the center,
wrinkled near the edges,
ragged on the outside.
I can force myself to see only the clear,
I can focus my eyes on the middle,
the essence,
the point from which clarity comes.
I can mix-match my memories with the breeze of my whisper
and smooth out the edges,
if I need to,
if I want to,
if my outsides get too frayed.

I do not suppose the teenage years are smooth for anyone, but for me they were enlightening and intriguing times, if not always easy and carefree. It was a simple, yet rich experience; a big box of riddles wrapped up in innocence. Cognitively, I know that I was aware of the unique attributes I apparently shared with no one, but somehow this reality never hurt my heart nor bothered my mind. I did not care that I lived within a different set of assumptions and neither did my friends. The art of friendly acceptance gave us each a warm canvas to explore.

I recall my high school classmates had at least three general groups we could identify with. I imagine there were others. As I think of them now, it occurs to me each was defined according to shared interests, a dream come true for AS people. I can easily bring to mind the group I was in. My crowd was filled with athletes, cheerleaders and student government leaders. I had fallen into this particular group while I was still in elementary school, years before we had any inclination of who we would be or what we would do in high school. Our friendship was a known quantity. It was something safe and dependable, qualities that can be in short supply for teenagers. We were the outspoken group, the one that asserted itself on everything both tangible and intellectual. Nothing went by us without first having to circumvent an opinion or ideology that we had planted squarely in its path.

It was easy for me to give my opinions on things, virtually all the time. I was by far the most blunt and outspoken of our group, even when my friends suggested I had gone too far. I never knew how far was too far. Even now, I cannot find one reliable reason for keeping my thoughts to myself. The world seems fickle on this point. Sometimes people want an opinion, sometimes they do not. Sometimes they say something so incredible an opinion has to be given. Other times they sit in silence seemingly unaware of the situation that lies before them. The entire dichotomy is too confusing. I do not see how anyone can ever know with any degree of certainty when they should voice their thoughts and when they should keep them silent. Sure, I often find myself wondering if I have said too much or worrying that I may have been misunderstood. Sometimes I even wish I had not said what I did. But I realized long ago that it would be easier for me to stop a dog from going after a bone, than it would be for me to stop my thoughts from escaping my mouth.

If giving an opinion had been all I felt I needed to do in high school, I imagine I would have gone to bed every night happy with every one of my days. I usually wanted more for myself, not because I intended to prove anything to anyone and not because I had set a series of goals I needed to achieve. I simply enjoyed certain activities and sought ways to explore them. Three particular activities caught my fancy when I was in high school. The first was competitive swimming. Water continued to enchant and calm me. Too bad it could not make a good swimmer out of me. I naively assumed that because I liked to swim, I would be a good team swimmer. I was wrong. In some ways I was a natural swimmer. I could hold my breath for very long periods of time, I had strong legs for kicking, and I was aerobically fit. But I failed in all the ways that really counted. I could swim for hours, so long as I was moving both arms together and both legs together. But I suffered miserably when a stroke required me to use bilateral coordination and balance. For instance, if I had to pull with my left arm, I could not coordinate a kick from my right leg. My swim coach gave up on me about as soon as she first saw me try to swim. She did let me stay on the team, however, and she even gave me the same workouts the other members had. My coach was never cruel or rude to me. How could she be? I was invisible to her.

I tried as hard as I could to keep up with the other swimmers. I arrived to practice earlier and left later, but I was not capable of teaching myself what I needed to learn. I went to a few meets with the team, but I never understood the social aspects of the group's dynamics. I sat alone at the meets, watching the clock until it was time to leave. I do not think anyone missed me when I quit the team. I cannot say I missed them either. What I missed was the water.

I dream sometimes that I had been coached by someone who was more sensitive to individual needs, someone who would have recognized my coordination problems as more than an example of a child who simply was not an athlete. At the very least, I wish someone had helped me more. But high school was in some ways a survival of the fittest. Only those students with extreme special needs were typically identified and assisted. Everyone else was left to find their own way. After I faced the fact that I would not be a winning swimmer, I found my way to the marching band's drill team, but not as a musician. I was a pep squad dancer. What a ridiculous choice for me to have made. How could I not have known that the same bilateral problems which kept me from being a good swimmer would also keep me from becoming a good cheerleader?

When we practiced for dance performances, it was common for one of the captains of our squad to face the rest of us while she showed us our routine. I do not know how they managed, but it seemed like everyone but me could tell their body to move in the opposite direction of what they were seeing, so that if the captain moved her left arm, they did too. I did not. When someone facing me moved their left arm, I moved my right arm. When they moved their right arm, I moved my left arm and so on and so forth. I knew all along that I was making a mistake, but no matter what I did and no matter how many times I told myself things like 'her right arm equals my left arm', I could not transfer the knowledge to the movement. After a few weeks of bilateral torture, I figured out I might find some success if I practiced our dance steps from the back row; a vantage point that allowed me to carbon copy the people who were facing the same direction I was. Eventually, after hours and hours of practice, I could make myself perform the dance steps with some degree of proficiency, if there was someone in front of me to give me cues. Of course, this was not the only talent a dancer needed. Part one was memorizing the steps to the routine, part two was synchronizing them to music. Part one was a breeze compared to part two. I was always off beat, always the girl begging to stay in the last row even though I was not the tallest, and I was always the girl who tripped.

I never mastered the aptitude of dance in high school, for precisely the same reasons I never mastered the step and dance aerobic classes that came into popularity after I was out of high school. The difference was, by the time I reached adulthood, I knew the odds were against me being able to do anything that took coordination. I did not recognize how deeply rooted my simple dexterity problems were when I was still a teen. But maybe that was for the better. I would not have tried half the things I did, if someone or something had told me I was bound for failure. I think it was a good thing I was too egocentric to think along those terms. As it happened, I eventually found success in an activity that charmed, interested and fulfilled me. I found the speech and dramatic arts club.

I think cultural and performing arts types must be Aspies. If not, they are surely the next best thing. They are at least amenable friends of Aspies. I found great acceptance among my drama peers, most of whom were extremely tolerant and appreciative of diversities and personal visions. I was able to flourish in such a warm and supportive environment, finding it to be the best place for me to turn many of my AS traits into real and viable assets. In those classes I was inspired by other eccentric thinkers who taught me to think of language as more than a means for expressing simple needs. Finally, I had found a natural place for me to be.

Linguistics and the act of speaking itself, have always been amongst my keenest interests, but I did not become immersed in the treasures they awarded until I studied them in high school. Words, and everything about them, hold my concentration like nothing else. On my over-stuffed bookshelf sit several thesauruses, a half dozen dictionaries, famous quotations books, and a handful of personal reflection journals. Language appeals to me because it lends itself to rules and precision even more often than it does to subjectivity. Put together in the right sequence, taking into account things like tone, perspective, implications and intent, a writer can tweak and bend words until they say precisely what they should. I am fascinated with the opportunities words provide. I love everything about them, especially the power they yield. Some words can please my eyes, given they have the symmetry of line and shape I favor. Other words can fascinate me by the melodies they sing when they are spoken. Properly handled – with care most of the time – words can work miracles on my sensibilities and on my understanding of the world, because each one has its own personality and nuance and its own lesson to teach.

Sometimes, the care I give to words can throw me into an obsessive compulsive ritual. I typically end up spending far too much time selecting which word to use and too much time reworking a sentence so that it looks and feels and sounds right. This all translates into a fixation that can grind my thought process to a halt. When I get like this, I cannot concentrate on anything else, not a thing, until I have found the perfect term or phrase I need. This tendency can make my experiences with the written word tedious, at least in terms of time and other missed opportunities, but never meaningless or futile.

Fine things happened when I mixed my voice with the monologues and original oratories I wrote. I would play with my voice, working it, pushing it to reach new tones and pitch, different volumes and a myriad of rhythms. I enjoyed the feeling my voice left on my ear, the way it resonated in my throat and the sensation it created as it slipped past my lips. My voice did as much as my thoughts to choose the words I would put in my work. I would search long and hard to find words that tickled, words that had smooth textures, and words that warmed when I spoke them. I knew I had written something great when I found words that looked, sounded and felt good. And when I knew I had something great, I performed well enough to routinely finish in the top five per cent of the competition.

Even though my public speaking competition days are behind me, I still work my voice, albeit in a different fashion. I have developed a habit of mimicking other people's speech, especially if their voice has heavy nasal or high shrill qualities, or extreme eastern or southern accents. I find I have to mimic these voices, otherwise they sting my ears like a wet towel slapped against my eardrum would. When I mimic agitating voices, I can play and replay them until I manage to edit them into a medley I can appreciate and value.

Most of my public speaking fell under a category called radio and television. Basically, I would sit behind a microphone and read news copy I had written, to a panel of judges. When I competed in this context, I usually won or finished in second place. There is no question that this was my favorite thing to do, but I also liked performances that challenged my nonverbal expressions and my body posture. It was great fun to think of myself as a doll I could bring to life. I enjoyed methodically planning how I could make a script or poem more meaningful with facial expressions and eye contact and the wave of a hand or the shift of my weight. It was like a puzzle I could piece together. Little did I realize it was also a wonderful way for me inadvertently to learn how to use my nonverbal communication skills when I was not presenting a piece of literature. I was coming to understand that words on paper sometimes had to scream to be heard, but that words spoken with a distinct voice and compelling expressions could whisper, for the combination was that powerful.

I never experienced apprehension or fear when I spoke in public. I do not understand why so many people do. I wonder if I am missing something, if I am overlooking some obvious problem with public speaking that falls beyond my grasp. Maybe I enjoy speaking in front of a group because it is a one-way communication experience and, as such, something that is not affected by the complications of other people's body language and non-verbal styles. Given a chance, I would much rather speak to a large group than I would to an individual or two. Small group conversations make my nerves feel like they are wearing stilts on an icy pavement. When I talk to other people, I have trouble following conversation transitions. I step on other people's words, stumbling ahead with my own thoughts, in almost every conversation I have. It was not like this when I performed monologues and oratories. It was easier. I never stumbled a bit. Standing on stage was a release for me, even though I was always a solo performer and so, on my own each and every time. It was as if all the thoughts I kept trapped throughout the day, all my weird observations on life and my strange obsessive wonderings, could leave my conscious and find a new home within someone else's mind. Once my thoughts were spoken aloud, I could finally move on to another thought or concern.

Speech competitions taught me a great deal about myself, especially when I was off the stage. On stage, I could try on the entire range of human emotions, even the emotions I typically had nothing to do with, and then as easily as I slipped them on, I could take them off and re-shelf them until the next time. But offstage, I did not have the luxury of pretending. I remember the first time I knew there was a vast difference between what I was able to make myself do in front of an audience, and what I could coax from myself when I was left without the stage lights. When I had to be me around peers I had not known for a long time, especially peers I was meeting for the first time, I froze.

Hindsight tells me this was AS nagging my reality, bubbling up and over until it became a cold, wet hand that held my calm to an ice tray white with frost. Try as I might, I could not sneak back and forth between the world of the normal and the world of the irregular. I seemed to shout my arrival the moment I made it to one place or the other. When I visited normal, I was relatively sure of myself and largely able to maintain my sense of composure, despite the fact I worried all along that eventually someone would discover I was an outsider. But when I side-stepped my way to the irregular, the glue that held me together softened and I melted a bit. Suddenly, without any kind of warning, my nerves would jump to center stage and demand my attention, making it impossible for me to remember any of the interpersonal speaking techniques and body language expressions I could show on stage. Something odd would happen to me and I would retreat into the places I used to visit when I was a little girl. I would turn my mind from everything that was going on around me, even the laughter and the jokes, the friendly discussions about everyone's upcoming events and the well wishes that were coming my way. I would concentrate instead on blanking out my thoughts, counting over and over and wishing I was in a still spot away from the noise. Maybe I was experiencing sensory overload. Maybe I was frazzled because I did not have any way of predicting what would come next. Or, maybe I simply felt uncomfortable sharing close space with people so foreign to me. All I know for certain is that these moments were terrible. Faces began to merge together, voices sounded out of sync and my perception fooled me. Things ran on slow speed then, letting an eternity slip by until I could find a quiet corner or an empty room to gather myself up again. It was hard to make me right at that point, but given time, I always did.

It is tempting for me to reexamine that period according to the knowledge I now have, and each time I do, I find myself wondering if I might not have learned more if I had not isolated myself from my peers. Would I have learned more useful information about personal interactions if I had been a part of a drama team instead of a solo act? Would I have come to realize that emotions and expressions and words are empty if they are not shared and received? Would I have been able to see, years before I finally did, that communication does not rest against a flat surface, but that it has a vivid, virtually three-dimensional element to it? I can only wonder…

The study of all things linguistic was clearly one of my favorite obsessions, but it paled in comparison to the fixation I kept on the wild western frontier and Hollywood's romantic comedies. When I was not watching the movies on television, looking through my vast collection of movie magazines or one of the dozens of books I had on the history of film, I was usually turning the pages of every fiction and nonfiction book I could find on cowboys and train robbers and American Indians and pioneers and western settlers. I loved anything to do with the way America lived in the late 1800s. I rode my horse bareback because that was how native Americans rode. I bought a cowboy hat with my first babysitting money. I even inquired into my genealogy to see if I was related to the infamous gambler and gun fighter, Doc Holliday. Other girls in their teens did not seem to share my interest in the old west, but then, neither did the boys. Not that any of them seemed particularly put off when I went on and on about how fascinating those times were. They were politely tolerant, but not inclined to add much to the conversation. After a while, I stopped trying to talk to my friends about my favorite topics, but I never stopped thinking about them or enjoying them on my own. I went to see western movies and old films by myself, not giving one moment's thought to the notion that this was an uncool thing to do. I made audiotapes of western television series and played them over and over instead of listening to the radio. I wandered the archives of the library all alone, never dreaming of asking someone else to join me in searching the stacks for books about Annie Oakley or Wild Bill Hickock or Sitting Bull. And I argued with my teachers when they tried to convince me to read something other than western lore, telling them it was my goal to read every book in the library on every western character I could find. I think I did.

I mark my growing obsessions in my own interests as the point when I should have begun to lose my footing in the friendship circles I called my own. I am amazed my peers put up with me and my peculiarities. Truth be known, they may not have, had it not been for a very good friend of mine named Craig. This friend was very bright and very funny and very well-liked. With him by my side, I was given an instant elevated status among our group and even beyond. He had been my friend almost forever and over the years he had become almost like a guardian to me. I do not know if he knew the struggles I faced when I tried to accomplish social skills without the benefit of some kind of direct instruction, and I do not know if he understood there were knots in my belly when I was around new people or faced with new situations, but I do know that he was somehow always there for me whenever I found myself swimming upstream or feeling penned in. In subtle and overt ways, he would show his support for me by saving me a seat at lunch, walking me to class, or picking me up to take me to a party. He fixed me up on dates, made me laugh when my nerves started to twitch, and kept me company if I was all alone in a crowd. He even came with me on a family vacation once when the person I had invited to come along had to cancel. Craig jumped in to my rescue even before I knew I needed to be rescued.

My friendship with Craig was perfect for me, it worked. I am good with friendships that allow me the freedom to assert my differences. I am comfortable and content with a few friends who know me well and understand my nuances. But I rarely remember a time, best friends in the background or not, when I did not prefer to be alone. Unlike most people I knew, I did not grow up feeling the need to make deep and strong connections with others. I do not think I ever consciously sought a friend or disregarded a friend. I was nice to people I knew and friendly to people I only passed in the halls. I was particularly good at fast bits of witty conversation, the kind of quick retorts that sounded more like a monologue I had snared from drama class, than a two-way conversation.

Overall, I think I would say I was rather perfunctory about my relationships with peers. In reality, they were not too awfully important to me. Not that I did not like the people in my group, I did. It was just that I would not have been terribly upset if I had been all alone and without a group to identify with. My own conversations and thoughts were always my best friends. I was happy spending time with only me, happy to talk to myself and happy to entertain myself. I think the only reason I ever invited a friend to come spend time with me was because my parents suggested it and because I knew it was something friends were supposed to do. I knew how to follow the rules of the teenage jungle, exactly like I knew how to follow the rules of baseball.

I was very conscious of the rules my friends set for themselves and the group, particularly as they applied to behaviors and other social skills. As if I had a Rolodex in my mind, I would categorize the actions of people, noting their differences and subtleties with a mix of abstract appreciation and real curiosity about why they acted as they did. I became very aware of the smallest and most subtle aspects of my peers' movements. I took note of how they threw their long hair over their shoulders, or tucked their bangs behind their ears or how they turned the whole presentation into an art show with braids and bows and curls. I mentally recorded the way they used their eyes, how they would open them wide when they spoke loud and animated, or how they would cast them downwards if they spoke quietly or slowly. I was captivated with the way their hands moved when they spoke, how they would bend them into shapes that looked like little buildings or twirl them about as if the hands were the message. I watched people like a scientist watches an experiment. Never did I feel like I was looking in a mirror. Always did I feel I was here and they were there.

Just as I took good notes on how people acted, so too did I make mental notes of how they dressed. Fashion trends have always diverted me, though I have never been able to understand them as entities deserving of a life filled with purpose. I was able to tell that my peers took their clothing choices seriously because everyone copycatted everyone else's style. I knew I was supposed to follow the rules set by fashion but try I as may, I broke them all the time. I still fought with textures and colors and patterns, like I did when I was a child and I simply could not bring myself to wear certain clothing no matter how many rules I knew I was breaking. Tight jeans that fell to the hip, shirts that were the color of clay, coarse wool jackets that wore the back of my neck raw…they were not for me. I settled for coloring a smidgen outside the lines, finding a handful of outfits that blended in well enough to avert stares, but not so well that I was miserable in them. And if those almost-trendy clothes of mine were dirty, I would wear whatever I happened to grab from my drawers even if what I had selected did not look well together. Not that I noticed. I designed myself for comfort and convenience, not trends.

This drove my girlfriends beyond distraction. They were forever advising me to pay more attention to my appearance. They would take me in the bathroom and give me hints on how to wear make-up and how to fix my hair. They would remind me how gross it was for me not to shave my legs or tuck my shirt in or wear the same outfit several times in one week. And they particularly hated my shoes, but not as much as I hated having my feet bound up in the stiff canvas of tennis shoes, or the slippery leather of dress shoes. To beat that feeling, I wore house slippers to school. I thought they were rather interesting little shoes and I saw nothing wrong with them, no matter how loudly my friends protested.

As long as things followed a set of rules, I could play along. Rules were – and are – great friends of mine. I like rules. They set the record straight and keep it that way. You know where you stand with rules and you know how to act with rules. Trouble is, rules change and if they do not, people break them. I get terribly annoyed when either happens. Certain things in life are givens. 'Thank you' is followed by 'You are welcome'. You hold doors open for other people. The elderly are treated with respect. You do not cut in front of other people, you stay in line and wait your turn. You do not talk loud in libraries. Eye contact is made when you talk to someone. The list goes on, but the intent never changes: rules are maps that lead us to know how to behave and what to expect. When they are broken, the whole world turns upside down.

If all teenage rules had been open and shut cases grounded in right and wrong, I am inclined to believe I might have slipped through my high school years uncharted and unrecognized as someone who saw things so differently. But as I have discovered, most rules fade the moment they inconvenience someone. With broken rules forcing cracks in my boundaries, I was left to develop my own. My rules were different than any I had memorized before. My rules allowed me to set my own trends and my own pace. They also allowed me to showcase some of my less obvious differences.

As I went through the motions familiar to many teenagers, I came to notice that everyone had some odd little habit they used in times of distress or absentmindedness. I noticed the nail biting, the lip biting, the hair chewing and the tiny muscle twitches. I heard friends humming to themselves, sucking their teeth, and tapping their feet. I knew there were all kinds of rules that people followed in order to calm themselves or occupy their time, but I think my favored habit was unique, at least among my friends. I had a preoccupation with round numbers, even though I hated and was terrible at math. Eventually, I incorporated that fascination into little chains of behaviors I would repeat by the tens. I rode my bike ten miles a day, exactly ten. Not one bit over or one bit under, even if I had to carry my bike up the driveway or ride it in circles in the garage, until I hit the ten mile mark square on my mileage counter. I also exercised around the count of ten. I might have bounced up and down in my pool one in ten groups of ten or I might have completed ten sets of ten movements for ten different calisthenics. I used to spin in a circle on my swing, stopping after I had gone around ten times. I took ten steps to make it up any set of stairs, skipping or repeating stairs, as I needed to so that I would come to the top on the count of ten.

It would be years before I would come to realize I did, and thought, many, many things that others apparently did not. When I was in high school, I was only beginning to see how peculiar my world was – not wrong or embarrassing or unessential – just peculiar and different. I was okay with that, then. I never minded standing aloof or apart from the crowd. I never felt lonely. My friends never pushed me aside, or forgot me, or kept themselves from me. People went about their business taking most things in stride.

My teenage memories are stuffed with good times and good people. Even when I start to remember something raw and ugly that might have tried to ravish me then, I am able to toss it off as a bad memory that had little effect on me. The experiences I had in high school prepared me for a bright future, for they gave me strength and insight and confidence to look at myself as an individual and not a parallel image. The only thing my close community of friends and teachers and counselors and mentors did not give me, the only thing they could not give me, was protection from the chill that would nearly undo me when I left them all behind.

3

Losing My Way

If I could, I would ask the world to make me skates
so that I could find its frozen water and set myself free
to smile, laugh, dance and cheer.

I'd see the boundaries that would be in a world frozen in
its place and they would keep me safe, away from
where the waters warm, away from the stares,
the thoughts that melt and the tears.

I would ask the world to skate with me, looking at the
gladness I had found, knowing, really knowing,
there was nothing left to fear.

I think that then we would all be free to live life as we
could, with more in common than apart, the fog would
lift,
the confusion would turn and true understanding
would hold us dear.

I do not want to write this chapter. It is uncomfortable for me to
think back on my late teens and early twenties. Hindsight has
taught me a few things about those years but it has not taken
away the bad memories or the deep embarrassment.

The future is often blinding for eighteen-year-olds, blinding
with unending brightness and possibility or blinding with a
potential to scorch and burn. Which experience is met depends
not just on the abilities or potential of the young person but so

very much on the support friends, family members, guidance
counselors, mentors, employers and continuing education
specialists legitimately offer. This is especially true for those with
any special need, even those whose needs are often invisible to
the unknowing observer. In my case, I seemed destined for a
future that was as bright as a star. My academic grades and high
IQ scores put me on a college and graduate school course early in
my high school years and by most standardized measures, there
seemed to be no reason to suspect I could not handle the demands
those goals would place on me. By the time I was ready to enter
college, I had received an academic scholarship, admittance into
every school I applied to and acceptance into every program I
wanted to explore. Objectively speaking, there was no reason for
anyone to suspect I needed special counseling or special tutoring
or mentoring. I did not seem to need anything more than the
typical college freshman needed – a stack of textbooks, a
rigorous academic schedule and a dorm room to call home.

Appearances can be deceiving. Somewhere along the line, I
became convinced that only large universities were worthwhile.
In fact I was so convinced, I gave up the academic scholarship I
had been offered by an excellent small private school and
enrolled in my state's major university instead.

This was my first mistake. The confusing, rambling, crowded
and expansive campus assaulted my limited sense of direction,
making it extremely difficult for me to find my way – literally and
figuratively – around campus. I remember leaving a class totally
unable to discern which way I needed to go in order to follow the
most direct path to my next class. The crowds of students would
fill the doorways and the halls, giving me little time to grab hold
of my thoughts so that usually I would just follow the wave of
students out of the buildings, as if I knew where I was going.

Once the crowd thinned, I would try to get my bearings. I
would look for big landmarks like statues or unique pieces of
architecture and then plot a visual map anchored by those sites.
For example, I knew that when I left the building my Shakespeare

class was in, I would come to either a fountain, a street or a parking lot. From there, I could stop and decide which direction I needed to go to make it to my speech communications class which was across the street and through the quadrangle. So, if I found I exited the building near the fountain, I would turn right and there would be the street, but if I had exited by the parking lot, I would turn left and then find the street. After that, I knew to follow the sidewalk toward the downtown area until I came to a set of stairs on the left which led me to the backdoor of the building I needed.

Once inside the buildings, I had a heck of a time finding my way around. Normally I had to rely on trial and error unless the interiors had their own landmarks — art work, display cases, unusual paint scheme — I could use as visual cues. Most of them did not, relying instead on the same plain beige walls dotted here and there by identical looking bulletin boards that did nothing to help me out. I would know enough to understand which floor I needed to be on, but once on that floor, I would have to wander up and down the halls until I found my room by the number etched above the frame of the door. This normally meant that by the time I found my class, I would be at least ten to fifteen minutes late, wet with nervous sweat and anxious from bone to bone. At first I would attend the class even though I was arriving so late. But I soon found it very uncomfortable to walk into a room in the middle of a professor's lecture. I knew it was rude, I knew the professor thought it was rude and, worst of all, it made me feel hopelessly feeble minded. Sometimes, I would just sit in the hallways outside the class trying to listen in through the closed door. It was not long before I quit going to any class that I could not find within the ten minute period we had between the end of one class and the beginning of another.

I was aware I should have been attending every minute of my classes and yet, for one reason or another I did not. Though I was not to know it then, it seems obvious to me now that it was my AS behaviors which kept me from simple accomplishments like finding a classroom or sitting through a lecture. I was not simply a young college student interested in going through life at a casual pace without regards to outcomes and consequences. I think the person I used to be was unwittingly caught in a game of cat and mouse with AS. I was the scared mouse and my AS the unpredictable cat that would jump out at me when I least expected it and chase away any rational thought I might have been capable of. Time after time, I acted without giving one thought to the aftermath. I completely quit my biology class at mid-term, without one thought to the low grade I would surely get, the moment my professor set a formaldehyde soaked fetal pig in front me, because I could not tolerate the intensely invasive smell. I only sporadically attended my college algebra class, again without concern for my grade, because the instructor's voice aggravated me beyond my limits. And I dropped out of one of my favorite dramatic arts classes because the room we met in was dark, musty, windowless and creepy – the kind of room that begs to be filled with old boxes of discards, not young students.

My perception grew more clouded every day. A fog set and would not lift. Spatial difficulties, sensory dysfunction, poor problem-solving skills, over-reliance on my visual thought patterns – the AS kept finding me – even though I never realized it.

With my limited class attendance, my grades quickly plummeted. I knew this could only mean a crash course with disaster but I really did not know how to avoid it. I am not certain if special needs learning centers existed then, in the late 1970s and early 1980s, but I do know it never would have occurred to me to visit one anyway. Having never been identified as anything other than gifted, I had nothing to raise my suspicions, nothing to make me think I would benefit from study skills partners, peer mentoring, social skills counseling, or even career planning. I tried instead to manage on my own, even when my troubles continued to mount. The campus and my curricula might have been my most obvious stumbling blocks, but they were not the cause of my worst memories. I think I could have survived as most college students manage to do, if those had been the only kinds of problems I had to contend with. I imagine most students do poorly in at least a few of their courses and I am positive there are many who never quite adjust to living away from home and everything familiar. My real difficulty came when I began to tell myself my differences were not just superficial incidentals, but cracks in my dignity.

I was aware that college would bring many changes in my life. I knew the geographics and academics and amount of responsibilities and kinds of challenges would be different, but I never gave thought to how different the social life would be. I had no way of knowing that AS left me without an intrinsic awareness of what it means to make and keep friends, to fit in and mold, to work cooperatively and effectively with others. Most people who come from supportive families learn to jump from their childhood to their young adulthood as if they are on a trampoline. They have the neurological balance to be buoyant and carefree, so that as they move through their experiences they can bounce here and there, making mistakes along the way with the certain confidence that they will be given an opportunity to land on their trampoline and bounce right back up to begin again. People struggling with Asperger's often find there is no trampoline to catch them as they fall, no soft and pliable cushion to propel them back to the beginning for a new and improved, better prepared jump. AS makes it difficult to learn from where you have been. It makes it difficult to generalize and problem solve. Without a built-in springboard to catch you as you fall and encourage you to try again, Asperger's people often find they fall to the hard ground, damaged and broken. I remember too many times during my college years when I did just that.

I must have thought the people I would meet in college would fall into my life just like those from my hometown did. But what I never included in my grasp for understanding was the fact that my hometown was more than a group of randomly placed people. It was a group of cohesive friends who had learned, over the course of a good many years, to accept one another for all our quirks and idiosyncrasies. I gave no thought to the possibility that I would move to school and end up any differently than I had ever been, a well-received young woman with some strong academic skills and the respect of my peers. I had no way of knowing college students would be so cruel to those who did not fit in the circle of their normal.

The spring before my freshman year was to start, I began to get recruitment letters from a variety of social and academic sorority organizations, no doubt because of my high academic marks. I took no real interest in the letters, other than to think to myself how odd it was that people so often choose to live and work in groups or packs of people. I had no intention of joining any group, other than as a casual member who would follow the line just as I always had, when I wanted to or felt I needed to. For the most part, I was interested in finding a few friends mostly out of curiosity, but also because I felt certain that once in the big world, I would find someone like me. Someone who shivered in crowds and closed their ears to noise. Someone else who could get lost in their own backyard. Someone who only wanted to go to the library or ride bikes with me every now and then. I just knew college would be a liberating experience that held no absolutes and no single files. I had a suspicion the members of sororities and most organizations were too much like lemmings for me, but I never begrudged them their existence or their lifestyle. I never knew how important memberships were. I thought I would find a friend or two without any kind of membership card. I underestimated the significance of belonging.

I did not expect much from my social life at college. I did not need much. I was accustomed to defining friendship in very simplistic terms. To me, friends were people I enjoyed passing a few minutes or a few hours with. I may not have known their names, but I did know their faces and a few of their interests and usually a thing or two about their routines. For instance, if I ran into the same girl every day on my way to class and if I knew she was interested in a speech communications degree and from the same part of the state I was from, I considered her to be a friend. Never a best friend or someone I felt compelled to do things with, but none the less, someone I could smile at or talk to for a few minutes on the way to class. Maybe even someone to go to the library with or eat dinner with. I did not need anything more, and I never really expected anything more. At first, this seemed to be all other freshman needed or expected, too. But as the first semester moved on, I seemed to be left behind. I noticed groups forming and all of them without me. I noticed people who I thought reminded me of people I had gotten along with from home, but they did not seem to notice me.

Soon, I found that my smiles were unreturned, my steps were never followed and my phone was never called. Soon, I saw I was invisible. On one level, this did not bother me. I liked my time alone and my personal space. But, day in and day out, rejection began to lay heavy on my shoulders most likely because I did not understand why I was being excluded. To choose to be left out is one thing, but to be locked out, is quite another. A smile and a few minutes of conversation used to be enough to make a friend, and for the life of me, I could not figure out when or why this had stopped being the rule.

By the second semester, I began to feel too detached, too close to lonely. It made me very angry to learn this. I had always known I did not think like other people and I had plenty of moments in the past when my differences kept me isolated and oddly desolate, but I knew how to fix those problems. I would just go to school the following day and talk to the person I sat next to and within no time, I would feel much better. I could not do that in college, no one would let me. I hated the fact that people were getting to me like this. I hated the influence others were beginning to have on my life. This was not like me. I had never cared before.

I wonder now, if my AS was beginning to fade then. If my sudden exposure to a world of change was somehow responsible for making me come face to face with the variances that altered the way I saw things, the way I thought. Without the protective attention of my childhood friends and family, I was bound to fall flat on my face. Perhaps this is what I needed to do. If I had not fallen, I might never have discovered how to nurture the parts of me that needed enriching... I might never have discovered how lucky I was to live in a kaleidoscope world...

I was beginning to see that I might never find my place in the big world, but I could not fathom why or what to do about it. I decided I would do the one thing I knew guaranteed a college student their rite of passage. I decided to join a campus social organization.

As luck would have it, a friend of mine from home invited me to try out for his fraternity's Little Sisters program. I think he knew I was drowning before his very eyes and he was trying as best he could to help me survive. I also think he knew that, by then, there was not a great deal he could do for me. Still, he was very sweet and kind and made all the arrangements for me to meet him at his fraternity house where I would begin the first stage of try outs. I went along with the idea, even though the entire concept upset my sensibilities, leaving me to feel like a toy high on a shelf who winds down each night with the wish that some caring soul will soon take pity and come to the rescue. I remember preparing for the event. I remember walking into town to find a dress, milling around amidst the confusion that always struck me in busy stores. Nothing looked good to me, nothing seemed to fit right and no matter what I put on, nothing hid the ten pounds I had gained. I ended up purchasing a dull grey dress with burgundy trim that made me look more like a school teacher than a college student. No matter, I thought. The important thing was, I had found something to wear beyond my daily outfit of choice. A pair of overalls and a man's flannel shirt.

My friend brought me to the party and did his best to help me fit in, but as a new member of the fraternity, he had other responsibilities. I was largely on my own from beginning to end. I keenly recall feeling like I was a particularly unwelcome intruder who had no business being at that event. I remember struggling with myself, begging myself to go shake a hand or start a conversation, but I could not bring myself to do either. I noticed how effortlessly the other girls seemed to be handling the crowd of young men. I noted too, that they were not shaking hands nor conversing very much at all. They were giggling and laughing and tossing their hair behind their shoulders, gently putting their hands on the boys' arms, looking totally lost in the limelight of the attention they were getting. I could see their formula but I could not bring myself to follow it. Slowly, the room began to accept some as its own, while it tossed the others aside. I watched as a few of the fraternity members made their way to a couch in a quiet corner or to the hallways that led to their rooms. I saw a few girls smile and say thanks and wander toward the door that would take them home. I remember feeling like a scientist who was curious to see who made it and who did not, but only after my friend came back to check on me, did I realize that I was standing completely alone, virtually twenty feet or more from the small circles and large groups of chatting and laughing people. Only then did I realize that I had been tossed aside.

A month or two later I ran into a few of the girls I recognized from one of my classes. Much to my surprise, they were enthused to see me and interested in talking with me. I recall feeling flattered by the attention, and glad to have their company – the loneliness was beginning to hurt my heart. The girls asked if I would like to go shopping with them, an activity I did not relish, but a date I was happy to make nonetheless. They gave me the time and place to meet them, asking me if I wouldn't mind driving because they did not have cars on campus. I told them I would be happy to do so, particularly since I always preferred to be the driver. I spent all week trying my very hardest to roust something from my closet that would pass for college cool. I settled on a pair of blue jeans and a sweater, the only real option I had outside of my overalls and the dress I wore to the fraternity party. I thought I looked about as normal as any other student, at least I was dressed like one and that, I assumed, was about all I needed to bring me to a successful day with my new friends.

Finally, the day came for the big shopping event and sure enough, the girls were waiting for me just like they said they would be. We found my car and I told them I would take them anywhere they wanted to go, explaining I never shopped in town much and had no real preference for anywhere in particular. The girls directed me to the middle of the downtown shopping area which kept me from having to admit I found it so difficult to make my way around town. I found a parking spot in no time at all, and after a few attempts even managed to parallel park my car. All was going great until we got out. The girls turned to me the moment we stepped on the sidewalk and told me to be sure to meet them back at the car in three hours. Then they turned to one another, began a new conversation and walked down the street…as far away from me as they could possibly go. I wish I could say I left the girls stranded where they had left me. But of course, I did not.

If this adventure had been a one-of-a-kind trip, I might not even remember it today. Unfortunately, the entire year was pelted with episodes just like it. Most were even more embarrassing and are more painful to recall. I think the real problem laid just below the surface of another of my most mysterious and difficult AS traits – my inability to understand my peers' conversations. I understood their language, knew if they had made grammatical errors in their speech, and I was able to make replies to anything that was spoken to me; but, I never came to hear what they were really saying. I never understood their vernacular. Suffice to say that, at that point, I was unable to read between the lines. Subtext and innuendo may as well have been birds flying by my window. It was frustrating being unable to break into the thought processes of my peers but I was more upset when I came to discern I never learned from one experience to the next. I kept falling into the same kinds of traps, even after my father warned me it sounded like people were only using me, even after I discovered it was an acquaintance from high school who had stolen my bike, even after I overheard a girl from my dormitory tell her boyfriend I was a fat slob. No matter what I saw or heard, I failed to get the message. I was not fitting in.

When summer break came, I went home defeated and frustrated. My grades were barely passing marks, my sensory dysfunction was turning my footing to mire and I had not found one single person who was like me. If I had, I might have felt normal.

Life at home was no easier or better for me than college was. By then, everyone I had grown up with was on a new track, headed for new goals and futures. I was glad for them, but awkwardly intrigued by their new lives. I did not understand how they were managing to do so well. How did they find their way when I lost mine? What did they have that I did not? Why were they happy and I so sad? Despite all the analysis I gave the matter, I found no answers.

My return to campus the next year was more obligatory than festive. I went back because I loved academics and knowledge and scholarship and research and writing papers. Despite all the rudeness and all the confusion, I went back to study and to learn. And for the most part, I was successful, except when I slipped back into the old pattern, the one that caught me when I was a freshman. The one that had no bright beginning... only a history of brittle endings. Yet when I was strong, I was very strong. And ever so slowly I began to find ways to help myself deal with the struggles I faced.

On a lark, I discovered I enjoyed working with clay and enrolled in a ceramics class for no credit just so I would have a legitimate reason to play with it. I remember the art lab like it was an oasis, especially in the late evening when it was almost always empty. It was wonderful then. It was so still and nice, so calm and uncluttered. And it was engaging. Without the hustle and bustle of other students, I could focus and relax and really enjoy the art. I could mush the clay and sculpt it into odd little shapes that paid no mind to anything real or recognizable. I did not care if I made tall pitchers or deep dished pie plates. I just wanted to work with the clay. It is the most simple and engaging texture I know.

The art lab was my favorite stop, but the architecture building was a close second. I was enthralled with the drafting classrooms, the slanted drawing tables, the straight edged rulers, the half mooned protractors, the steel compasses and the piles of fountain pens and mechanical pencils. I loved watching the students sitting at their tables, single bright lights focused over their shoulders, as they concentrated on their designs, so riveted and intent. I envied them their tools and their quiet and their skills. I would have given anything to have joined them, but I knew I did not have what it took to draw straight lines and tiny figures all the while contemplating difficult mathematical and engineering decisions that would need to be considered in the design. I wish I had gotten up the nerve to take an introduction to architecture class. It would have been dazzling to use their room and their gadgets, rather like I did the art studio – not for credit or great productivity, but for pleasure and enjoyment.

To this day, architectural design remains one of my most favored subjects and now that I am older I indulge my interest, giving in to the joy it brings me. In many ways it is the perfect elixir for whatever ails me. When I feel tangled and tense, I get out my history of architecture and design books and set my eyes on the kinds of spaces and arenas that make sense to me; the linear, the straight lined and the level buildings that paint pictures of strong balance. When I feel blighted by too many pragmatic mistakes and missed communications, I find my home design software programs and set about building a perfect sense home. There is something about the architectural design process that makes my brain click and fit.

As I began to find things that worked to balance my system, I found I cared less about the differences that kept me from figuring people out. Maybe I had just grown tired of viewing social skills as another academic class, a foreign language that I had to study, research and observe. Either way, I lost interest in the condition of humans, but I never lost interest in the human condition. I worried when I saw other students on campus who sat in the movie theaters by themselves, or played tennis against a backboard, or never smiled at anyone they passed. I had figured out by then that the friendship game was played by groups of snickering co-eds, not dispirited solo players. And I knew my own sensibilities were somewhere in between. When I walked or sat or did things alone, I did not hold my head down, slump my shoulders or wither away. I might have had knots in my belly thanks to some sensory dysfunction, I might even have been terribly confused or disoriented by what I was hearing, but I never felt or acted uncomfortable merely because I was alone. I knew there had to be a vast difference between my situation and those who looked so sad. It was then that I found a way to erase a bit of my loneliness.

Because I never needed, wanted or expected much from friends, I was the perfect friend for those who had no friends. My simple hellos or casual and short conversations, fit well with my peers who never fit in. Though we had different reasons for moving outside the big social circle, we were neighbors in isolation nonetheless. And so, I took it upon myself to offer tiny pieces of friendship, as best I could offer, whenever I could. I am not certain if the people I tried to gently befriend ever realized my concern for them. I do not know if I even helped them hold their heads a little higher. I do know they helped me. I felt good about myself when I received a smile in return for one I had sent. I was happy all day if I could get a lonely peer to talk to me in the cafeteria line. I was thrilled if my starting a conversation led them to continue it. I knew I had made a simple human connection, and that was all I needed.

My years in college would have presented the same kinds of havoc and distress had I gone straight to a vocation. The fact that I chose further education was not my problem. The things I could have avoided are generic and can be applied to any other AS person making their way through life. I know in my heart and in my head, that if I had owned more AS knowledge, if I had been able to objectively understand that terms like rigid thinking, semantic pragmatic disorder, social impairment, echolalia, bilateral coordination problems, sensory integration dysfunction and auditory discrimination, were very real words that defined who I was, I would have made small changes in my course. I would have gone to a smaller and perhaps more empathetic school. I would have realized I had a different set of needs and wants that set me apart from many of my classmates, but that never meant I was undeserving or incapable. And most important, I would have asked for the support I really needed.

I had convinced myself that my high IQ and high academic achievement record meant I was strong enough to handle whatever came my way. In reality, they only worked to help me fake my way to a false sense of security, a security that vanished and left me cold with fear the moment it was overwhelmed by the reality of my AS challenges.

I was hit hard when I had to realize smarts were not enough to make it in this world. I was turned upside down when I had to admit I could not find anyone who saw things like I did. I was crippled when I found out it took more than I had to give to make new friends. Looking back, it is really no wonder I was never able to build any friendships in college. I was not very good at figuring people out. And so it seems, no one was very good at figuring me out either. Without friendships, my version of friendships that is, I had very little support. Without peers to show me how to fit in and how to make the most of what I had, I could not stay connected. I foundered.

By the time I finished my first six years of college I was a bit beaten up, limping with failure, and deep in despair because I did not yet know why those things that came so seemingly easy to others, were so impossible for me to achieve. But I was not undone. My slow descent into total confusion and overwhelming anxiety attacks did lead me to a visit with a counselor on campus who gave me some of the best advice I ever received. She told me I needed to assess my strengths and weaknesses, to chart what I wanted to do and how I could do it, and to lay a plan for success that was reasonable and probable. And she told me something that probably seems even more filled with common sense than all the above thoughts combined. She told me I needed to get out in public more, to exercise in the fresh air, to find a job that might help me meet friends, to do the things I most enjoyed, to cultivate my interests and hobbies and most important – never to apologize for my imperfections or my idiosyncrasies. She reminded me in only a few hours of time together, that I was a capable woman who could do so many things with my life, if only I would learn to tame my life and make it work. Excellent advice for anyone, but lifesaving advice for someone with AS.

For years and years, I tried to pretend my college years were as tremendous as they were supposed to have been. I culled my memories for great times and stories and found ways to elaborate a few isolated examples into what would then pass for a myriad of good times. At first I thought I was kidding myself doing this, faking my way again. But I've grown more objective these past few years, and in so doing, I think I've been able to see those years through better vision. The things that I recall with disdain still leave a bitter taste in my mouth, but lately I have begun to find some memories that reveal a softer side of humanity. Looking far over my shoulder, I can call to mind people who must have been interested in my friendship. I can see a boy I knew as if it was yesterday. I can hear conversations we had and interests we shared. But more important, I can remember his face and the expressions he made as we talked. Today if he looked at me like he did then, I believe I would have seen the kindness and gentleness that was his. I never did much with this boy when I had the chance. I missed his offer of friendship. I would not miss that offer if it was made today. His face would make sense to me today.

I think back too, on a boy I dated during my last year in college when I was no doubt moving beyond the roughest parts of my young adult AS. He was the only close college friend I had. The only person who made his way through to me, no doubt after a long walk with patience that set him on a dogged determination to find out who I was. This friend found a way to meet me in my world, without making any demands that I meet him in his. Ironically, I do not even think he knew what he had done. To him I was a friend he liked to do things with, someone to share life with for a while. He never batted an eye when he saw I lived with two dogs and five cats, instead of a bunch of girls. He never expressed any concern over my weird habit of grilling people for way too much information. He always stood by me patiently when I freaked out from having had too much sensory stimulation. He never questioned me or criticized me, he just let me be. If only everyone could be that gracious – maybe then, we would not even need a definition for Asperger's Syndrome.

4

A Slow Walk Home

Will I know where to go if I find the way?
Will anything change or will things always be the same?
It doesn't really matter to me if I am here or there
or somewhere in between,
so long as I know where I am going.

When I hit my mid-twenties I was somewhere between the bright
new college graduate and the slightly off-beat lady who talks to
pigeons in the park. Truth is, I was both. By then I was fully aware
that I would need to mask myself, as best I could, according to the
set of circumstances that sat before me. I knew for instance, that I
could not talk to myself during a job interview. I knew I would
have to dress a certain way in order not to evoke long stares. I
understood that it was inappropriate around certain circles to
bring up the fact that my home was a zoo filled with dogs and
cats. I was beginning to see life more objectively, to realize that
though I did not see the purpose in most rules, or more important,
the harm in my breaking so many of them, I needed to follow
them as best I could. Occasionally I would find someone who
would let me make things up as I went along but for the most part
I knew people expected me to merge with them as
inconspicuously as possible. By my twenties I knew these
premises were true; trouble is, I still did not have the mechanisms
to comply as often as I might have.

Shortly after I completed my master's degree, I moved from
the relatively safe harbor of my college town to Houston, Texas;

an overwhelming city by anyone's standards. I had no plan when I moved there, no reason for being there, other than to be near my future husband – a plan that did little to prepare me for my life there. I think my new degree from college must have fortified me with flawed confidence leading me to think that if I could finish a post graduate degree, I could accomplish any goal I set my mind on, including living on my own in a rather foreign and engulfing environment. I remember thinking my degree would afford me a great deal of respect in the career market, though I had no idea which career I would ultimately pursue. I thought I would be welcomed by any number of professions, even those beyond my field of multi-media. I was more than naive. I was short sighted and still very vulnerable to the AS traits that kept me confused. Still, I was stronger than I ever had been, and so, not totally without reasonable odds for some kind of success. As it turned out, I was offered the first job I applied for, and though I did not know it at the time, it was probably the only job beyond freelance writing that would suit me well. Two weeks after I arrived in Houston, I accepted a job as an instructor at the University of Houston.

I do not know if teaching at the college level appealed to me more because of the freedoms it gave me, or because it did not require me to make much of a change in the routines I had established as a college student. Everything about teaching college classes was as good as or better than, the best parts of attending them. I liked the structure of the courses, but also the spare time in between. I enjoyed the studying and the lecturing and the new knowledge I found each time I turned a page in my textbooks. And I most enjoyed the very casual and temporary teacher-to-student relationships. They were the perfect kinds of friendships for me.

Everything about my job was darn near perfect, except for one crippling element – the school's physical location. Unfortunately, the campus I worked on was located in a terribly busy and overcrowded urban area; a nightmare I had to contend with day in and day out. I was never able to find my way to school without first getting lost in some capacity, be it driving the wrong way down a one way street or missing my exits or following the wrong detours. To make matters worse, I drove a mini-station wagon that did not have an automatic transmission or air conditioning; in other words, a vehicle that did very little to comfort me in the hot and humid Houston weather. All these elements forced my sensory integration dysfunction into a high state of chaos. Without fail, I would arrive at the university sweating, sticky, anxious, dazed and confused. Luckily, my interest in teaching students and the college campus environment usually carried me beyond the brink, so that after my sensory systems defrosted, I completely loved my job. Until the day everything changed.

In an attempt to avoid the tangled web of too many sensory overloads – the mass confusion and terrible noise that ride with traffic jams, the sticky weather, the worrying over getting to work on time – I decided to leave for the university at the crack of dawn. While this change in my routine helped me to avoid my most obvious paralyzing AS trait, it catapulted me directly into another AS trap. The trademark of AS. Social impairment.

I loved being on campus by 6:30 in the morning. I relished the emptiness of the university, the linear hallways that broke from their straight lines into square rooms with neat rows of desks and chairs. I liked the order that stood in the buildings when students were not filling them with gab and shuffling feet and too many patterns and colors. I liked the stillness. I also liked the solitude. In the hushed university, I unwound from the drive and let my ears rest on nothing. I relaxed. I felt safe and in control, soothed by the knowledge that my sensory system would eventually settle in response to the silence. I did not realize that though my sensory system was no longer vulnerable to an assault, the rest of me was.

I remember making my way to class one particular morning just as I always had, with my coffee raised for sipping, my paper

under my arm waiting to help me pass the time, and my fat
backpack laying its weight across my shoulders. With all my
objects in tow, I felt balanced and grounded. Normally, I would
have stayed that way – nice and balanced – until my students
came in. But on this day, I had a visitor. I recall sitting at my desk
reading the paper, when a man I had never seen before came into
the room. I noted the early hour but gave little thought to why he
might be on campus so soon before class was to begin. After all, I
did the same thing. I noticed the man was older than most of the
students and I remember thinking he was dressed differently
than the college kids tended to dress. He was not wearing jeans
or dressed as if he was looking for a date. He was dressed in
ragged, mud-colored pants and a too worn flannel shirt that
faded up and into his ashen, leathered face. Still, I was not
particularly alarmed, only annoyed by the look of him. I can still
hear the voice he used when he spoke to me. He spoke in a
monotone, keeping cadence with the pace his feet kept as he
slowly made his way to me. I had yet to stop and worry about his
presence in my classroom. I was more curious, more intrigued by
the effect he had on my quiet room, than I was by the possible
effect he could have on my safety. He told me he had been in jail,
that he had just been released. A tiny bell sounded in my thoughts
to alarm my suspicions, but I barely heard it. I was simply too
engrossed by his moldy appearance to make much of a decision
about his possible motives.

Ironically, though it was my AS that kept me from
understanding this man was oddly misplaced at the best, and
harmful at the worst, it was also my AS that helped me to realize I
was in trouble. The tiny bell turned into a blaring alarm the
moment he came within an arm's length away from me. I am
disturbed anytime anyone breaks my personal space rule, but in
this case, I was mortified. Not scared as much as disgusted,
though I might have been more frightened than anything else, if
he had not smelled so offensively. Logically, I think I always
knew he was not a student or just a friendly person who

happened by. I am sure I knew he was not someone I needed to be around. But until he and his smell aggravated my personal space, I really did not depend much on my logic.

The instant he violated my space, I backed up to move myself away from everything about his actions and his person that gagged me. Still he kept coming toward me, inch by inch, very slowly like a motion picture stopping at every frame. It never dawned on me to scream. It did not occur to me to run, though I never quit backing up. I do not think my feeble reactions were affected by a state of shock. I was conscious of the room, the stillness and the darkness outside and the fact that we were alone. I do not remember tasting fear the way I do when my children almost wander into a busy street or when I see a terrible accident almost happen. I think I was just unable to separate my sensible emotions from my sensory overload on that day; everything was too jumbled.

Thankfully, miraculously, a male student I had never known to be early before, came into the class and quickly and confidently walked to my side so that he was wedged between the man and myself. For some reason, the student's closeness to me did not offend me, but it did bother the man. In the blink of an eye, he disappeared out the door. When the man was gone from the room, I remember the student asking me if I was okay, if I needed anything, if the man had hurt me. I remember remaining very calm, almost wondering why he was so concerned, then I remembered the man's smell, his violating my personal space. Then, I knew I should have been afraid. I knew I had made a terrible error in judgement. I knew I had just been very, very lucky.

I took that experience with me like a student takes the knowledge he uses to pass an exam. I let it teach me a lesson about human behavior, one I was unable to know intrinsically. Never since then have I put myself in a position where I might be caught off guard. I still go many places alone, but never without looking for a quick exit, never without reminding myself that if someone does come too close I should scream, and never without telling myself there are people in the world who do mean to harm others. Lessons come hard sometimes, and sometimes, at a very high cost. The price I give to understand people is often more than I have to offer.

The experience at the university pointed out to me just how little I understood about human behavior. Objectively, I was able to see how close my inability to judge a person's motive properly had brought me to personal harm, but still I could not catagorize what made one person safe, another fun, another someone to build a relationship with or another someone to avoid. I did realize, by then, that there were some rules to friendships, some parameters that made them possible and sustaining, but I was still unclear as to what those rules and parameters were. To be perfectly honest, I remain confused.

After I quit the university, I took a job as an elementary education teacher. I enjoyed every second with the children and every aspect of teaching, but I was awkward around the adults I worked with. When I was with a group I would rather naturally resort to my stage talents. Literally. I smiled, made witty remarks and told interesting stories, and when I ran out of stories to tell, I left as if I was walking off the stage. I tried my very hardest to be a gracious and kind co-worker, but I never got the hang of it. I still do not. For example, I can never tell how much time needs to pass before I buy someone I have recently met a little 'thinking of you' gift. What if on the very day we met, I see something I think the new friend would like? Should I get the gift then and save it for say, six weeks, and then give it? Or can I give it away that afternoon? Or am I wrong about the whole gift concept. Is it just something commercials promote and not something I am really supposed to act on? Do I really have to talk on the phone to anyone if I think the conversation is boring or a waste of my time? If there is a lapse in the conversation, am I supposed to hang up or tell a joke or just sit there? What if I like the person well enough, but I decide I cannot stand one of their behaviors or habits? Can I tell them right away or do I have to wait a while, and if so, how long and if not, what am I supposed to do to keep from focusing on their annoying habit? The questions are endless, and the concerns mountain high. This is why human relationships usually take me beyond my limits. They wear me out. They scatter my thoughts. They make me worry about what I have just said and what they have just said, and how or if that all fits together, and what they will say next and what I will say then, and do I owe them something or is it their turn to owe me, and why do the rules change depending on who the friend turns out to be and…well, the whole thing drives me to total distraction and anxiety.

If I could have spent all my time and energies on my students, I think I might still be teaching. But of course, this could never have been. I had to interact with the administrators, counselors, parents and other teachers, no matter the discomfort. I never wanted to work on my teaching skills with my principal, relax with my co-workers in the teacher's lounge or talk to parents about anything other than their children. I had to force myself to attend staff meetings, hating the thought that I was expected to be a team player. I had to make myself join the faculty choir only because I knew it was expected of me. I had to will myself to smile while parents kept me after class with stories of their day or their goals in life. Thankfully, when I had to, I could appear interested, intrigued and motivated by the discussions and people around me. All I had to do was fragment myself. One of me could nod, interject and produce monologues of creativity. The other me heard only my inner thoughts, felt only my irritation at the situation, understood only the need to escape. Neither of me was very good at listening to entire dialogues, but both were very good at hearing the first parts of sentences or even words, and then disregarding the other halves.

It was not so much that people and their words and actions irritated or bored me; the effect was far more inclusive than that. People, particularly people I never saw or thought of unless they were sitting in front of me, unraveled me. They unhooked the calm in me and let loose too many thoughts, too many images, too many questions. My mind would melt amid the noise and the light and the voices and the asymmetrical patterns and the smells and the images, as I desperately tried to attach meaning to every word every person uttered. If I could not find a reason out of my meetings, and believe me I found many, I would allow my mind to settle on a few of my favorite obsessive rituals. I might have counted to ten over and over and over. I might have typed sentences in my mind, creating patterns as I did, so that my left hand would spell out the first two letters, then my right hand, then left, then right, until the sentence was spelled using a variety of symmetrical patterns. I might have ground my teeth to a rhythm playing in my mind.

I can imagine that other people have all kinds of masking rituals they do to pretend they are interested in the topic at hand, and so in that, I am probably not so very different from the norm. The difference comes, I think, at the point when closure comes. Speaking to others, I learned they quit their ritual the moment they want to, or the moment they need to. I go beyond that and continue my habits until their symmetrical pattern is complete or until the rhythm is over. I could not, and cannot, seem to easily shake my compulsive rituals from their hold on my thoughts. Not until they have completed their pattern. I try terribly hard not to fragment, particularly if I know I am going to be called on for much input or conversation. I know it is important to stay on task and work with others as well as I can. And for the most part, I can, at least on short projects. But back when I taught, I had to fight with myself to stay on track. I would try to keep my eyes very still, concentrating intently on people's faces, but not their gestures. Gestures took on dialogues of their own, making it even harder for me to keep up with the conversation. I would take notes, hoping that if I wrote down everything that was said, I could later piece everything together like a puzzle. Or, I would completely take over the meeting, asserting my own thoughts and ideas, as if

I were the self-appointed expert. But when all else failed, I used to rely on a 'fitting in' trick that is nothing more than a sophisticated form of echolalia. Like a professional mimic I could catch someone else's personality as easily as other people catch a cold. I did this by surveying the group of people I was with, then consciously identifying the person I was most taken in by. I would watch them intently, carefully marking their traits, until almost as easily as if I had turned on a light, I would turn their personality on in me. I can change my mannerisms and my voice and my thoughts until I am confident they match the person I wanted to echo. Of course, I knew what I was doing, and of course, I was somewhat embarrassed by it, but it worked to keep me connected and sometimes that was all that concerned me. It was simply more efficient for me to use the kinds of behaviors other people used, than it was for me to try and create some of my own.

Old habits are hard to break and sometimes I notice myself echoing even though I work at home now and rarely feel compelled to fit in at all. Interestingly enough, I do not think anyone else realizes I am echoing, not even the people I am copying. Everyone that is, except for those who know me quite well. A few very observant friends have noticed an occasion or two when I had lost myself in the shadows of someone else, but no one has ever noticed as quickly or completely as my AS daughter does. She recognizes the moment I bend my voice or my motions to match someone else's and it drives her to distraction. In no uncertain terms she will demand I stop acting like whomever, that I quit walking this way or that, that I stop pretending to be someone I am not. Though she does not yet fully understand the weight of her words, there is little that keeps me from comprehending the fact that she is right on track with her observation. Funny that she, another Aspie, is often able to see my pretence before I am.

I have come to the conclusion that even though I need to stop doing it, it is simply easier to echo, more comfortable and typically more successful superficially to pretend to be someone I am not. It is like putting myself on automatic pilot and free floating without lending a care to whether or not I am fitting in with the crowd. I must be if I am momentarily someone else. It's a free ride until someone else notices. But it is a ride I have decided I need to get off. And with the help of my daughter and a few of my closest friends, I think I will, mostly because when I am with the people I really understand, the people whom I trust implicitly, I never have to take a free fall.

The people who have proven they will stand by me no matter what I say, think or do, have given me a finer gift than they will ever realize. They have given me the real gift of freedom that allows me to experiment with my development as I continue to refine and sharpen my instincts and actions. These are the friends that do not wince when I fracture a social rule. The people who offer immediate dispensation should I offend them with my words or actions. The colleagues who call me to offer their support before I have a chance to tell them I am falling apart. I am aware these are the kinds of acquaintances everyone treasures, but for AS people, they are much more. They are our barometers and our mirrors. By their actions we see how we are doing and in their eyes we can find who we are.

My two closest friends, Maureen, who has known me almost forever, and Margo, who found me during the last part of my most obvious AS years, help me to know what acceptable is, not just because they are always willing to offer instructions on how to act or advice on how to perceive things, but more important because they are so loyal in their affirmations that I am fine just the way I am. Through their eyes I am perfectly fine. Each of them dismisses my idiosyncratic ways with a smile and a wave of the arm, as if to say, *You're okay. Keep your head up. You can do this.* They are confidence builders, confidants, cheerleaders, and advisors. They rein me in when I travel too far, they protect me from obvious blunders, and they applaud me when I stumble onto some part of me that is particularly worthwhile. But most important, most endearingly, they protect me, whether they realize it or not, from those who do not afford me so much grace.

They are quick to come to my defence, perhaps with just a word or a look, should someone begin to judge me for something I have said or done. And yet, they never condescend or patronize me. They simply illuminate that which is made better by my AS, my straightforwardness and assertiveness and creativity and tenacity and loyalty. Because they see me first as someone who possesses many good qualities, and only then as someone who is just a tiny bit different, they give me the notion to begin to see myself in that light as well. And though I cannot explain why this happens, their belief in me fosters my own belief in myself, which in turn helps me to become less apprehensive and more able. Maybe I just see myself as more able. Maybe I have just learned how to put my best foot forward in public. It does not matter what the reason, for the truth is, Maureen's and Margo's influence is substantial to my self-esteem, so important that when this invisible difference that is my walk with AS comes home to stay me, I am quickly comforted and buoyed by the fact that my friends will be there for me, no matter what, no matter where.

When I am with my closest friends, I can feel what it must be like to have a bunch of other friends, and for a moment I think I might just be over the old hang ups and anxieties. Sometimes, I will even try to do a really big friendship thing. I will host a lunch or show up at a function or even ask someone to go shopping with me. But, unless the person is extremely straightforward and blunt, I usually end up climbing back on stage, reciting the old lines and the old jokes, as my stomach starts to knot and my thoughts remind me how difficult this all is for me. I worry about this inability of mine, not so much because of how it affects me, but more because of how I think it might affect my children or the people whom I do not seem to grow close to. I do not want my children to grow up thinking they need to be loners, just because I am. I do not want the kids to be embarrassed because their mom would rather stay at home than join other moms for coffee or a girls' night out. And I do not want the people whom I meet to get offended if I turn down their invitations or never offer one on my own. I wish people could understand that I can soak up all I need from most friends in just a few minutes, then walk away happy and content, knowing I have just spent time with a friend. I am not trying to be at all evasive or unfriendly, I just fill up fast.

I like the friends I have, the few-minutes-a-day kind and the going-out-to-lunch-together kind. But I think it is important to acknowledge that there are many AS people who might never develop close friendships, even when they have learned how to be less egocentric, how to read nonverbal messages, how to express their wants and needs at the appropriate times and in the appropriate manner, and how to appreciate the nuances of proper friendship etiquette like secret keeping and personal space boundaries. I simply mean to say that truly close friendships are often very difficult to find, no matter who you are, and if I were counseling someone with AS, I think I would be very honest and objective about that possibility. I would try to explain that sometimes, no matter what we do and no matter how wonderful we might be, things happen to interfere with friendships. I would lead them, for example, through elaborated stories that illustrate people moving to far away towns, people getting wrapped up in their busy schedules, following different routines, having different interests, enjoying different kinds of play, and having their own set of difficulties and responsibilities. I would try to explain that sometimes time and place and sets of circumstances all work against real friendships. If this kind of open honesty is not a part of the total social skills counseling, I worry that an AS person's literal minded thinking might lead them to believe in a magic friendship equation that says *being nice + sharing toys + keeping secrets = friends and invitations to parties*. I worry, what will happen if the equation does not work out?

If it were me, I would want to make it very clear that life can be great with or without a large group of friends, but I would still try to help the AS person to understand that friendships come in many shapes and sizes, that they can be casual and brief, or if it turns out differently, strong and enduring. I think I would try to help them look for friendship circles that would be most likely to include people they would enjoy. People who share the same interests, ideas, morals, beliefs and general lifestyles. I would encourage them to join special interest clubs. I would advise them to cultivate a few moments with people they see in their neighborhood, at work, at school or on the regular routines. I might suggest they find a four legged friend to keep them company, not just for the therapy animals can provide, but also because pets can often bring out the best in all kinds of people and because they can bring strangers together. It is my opinion that with good and honest social skills training and follow-through counseling that works to help the AS person find appropriate social circles, all AS people can find friends. The question I cannot answer is, will they?

My deep, dark fear, the one that makes my bones scream, is that there are AS people in search of friendships who will never find any, no matter what they do, solely because of their AS. With those people on my mind, my heart breaks, for I know the reality that will wound them as they stumble forward, deeply lonely and ever more estranged from others. I hope that, as society continues to break the boundaries of normal, the boundaries so many cannot see and so many cannot find, this blight which robs good people of growth and happiness will ebb into a distant hollow, unseen and forgettable. And then, maybe then, the world really will welcome all people.

5

Crossing the Bridge

I mark my life by moments in time,
captured like morning glories at dawn,
small and simple, yet fine and real.
Moments define me, they make me complete.
I envision the times that come together to form who I am.
Each vison finds me nearing a bridge,
some slippery and unstable made of ropes and broken planks,
some certain and solid and well worn beneath iron gates,
all of them promising a worthy journey,
should I only have the will to follow their lead,
and my friend to hold my hand as I cross.

As most of my AS traits continue to fade away, I have noticed the most tenacious of the lot scatter like bubbles in the breeze, popping up here and there and usually at the most inopportune moments, teasing me from the thought that I will ever be anyone else's normal. Try as I might to catch and contain them, these are the qualities I will never lose and only rarely hide. I would not mind, so much, these reminders of my unique character, if they were of a different sort. For instance, I feel no shame over my poor spelling or my central auditory discrimination problems because the consequences they provoke are easily explained and largely benign. But when I discover I have let my guard down and wandered into a place that provokes my sensory integration dysfunction or my inability to cue in on someone's point of view – I lose my footing and find myself dizzy, shaken, nauseated and hot – acutely hot, so hot it hurts to touch my face or focus my eyes. When this happens, I desperately look for the only person who can almost instantly save me from reeling beyond control. I reach for my husband.

No matter how many times I say it, I cannot overemphasize how important a strong support system is for people with AS. Friends and family members are of course crucial members of that support team, but I have to think that the majority of influence comes most naturally from the person we with AS choose to share our lives with, that is *if* we choose someone. I marvel at those in the Asperger's community who find wonderful success seemingly without the support of someone close, for I know I would never have come this far if my husband had not been by my side. Not that our life together has always been easy. Like all married couples, we have had our share of problems, particularly when it comes to the one big issue that tears most marriages apart. The stuff of communicating.

By the time I met my husband I was pretty well convinced I would never understand anyone well enough to maintain something everlasting. The men I had been dating were nice men who shared some of my interests and hobbies, but with each of them there was always an unspoken and unseen something that stood between us – like the curtain that kept the truth of the Wizard from the people of Oz. I never gave much thought to what the curtain was hiding because when I did, it led me to distraction. I could not intrinsically or intuitively fathom what lay in the shadows, things I can now identify as the cornerstones for patience, flexibility, empathy and objectiveness. Before I came to terms with myself, these emotions were held at bay, nearly in my vision but just beyond my reach. It took years with my husband before I could swim to each one. Years before I could catch them and store them safely in my heart. My AS behaviors – the sensory integration problems, literal mindedness, perseverance and rigid thinking tendencies – acted like arrows tipped in poison that stood poised and ready to pierce every relationship I ever found.

From the moment I met Tom, I sensed he was a great deal like me. He had an interest in virtually all of my favorite activities, even my favorite pastime that no one else had ever expressed an interest in. Tom was just as enthralled as I was by university campuses...their architecture and structure, their quaint museums and galleries, their landscape and athletic stadiums, and their research libraries and bookstores. Later, it came as no surprise to me when he expressed an interest in becoming a college professor. The university environment is the perfect backdrop for his personality and mine. Many things caught our mutual interest, but virtually every one was linked by a common tie to solitude. Like me, Tom dislikes crowds and social gatherings. He does not care for environments that are charged with emotion or chaos, and he does not care how he fits in with the rest of the world. Like me, he is a loner. Quiet and calm became our glue. Now, I know that sounds simplistic and maybe even too subdued to act as a catalyst for togetherness, but in our case it provided a strong bond. To this day, it is the very element that draws us together even when we are at our worst.

When I try to list all the cracks in our communication, I immediately focus on how hard it is for me to follow Tom's logic. He is a man of few words and I require grand elaborations, well calculated metaphors and strong visual images to understand language. For instance, if Tom were to tell me he was disappointed he had missed me at lunch, I would wonder if he meant to say he was sad – which is simply regretfully sorry; unhappy – which is somewhere between mad and sad; disheartened – which is a lonely sad; mad – which makes you want to argue with someone over what they had done; angry – which makes you want to ignore the person you are feeling this way towards; furious – which makes you want to spit; or none of the above. In order for me really to understand what people are saying I need much more than a few words mechanically placed together. A succinct speaking and writing style is not nearly enough for me. Words by themselves are too vague. Rich elaborations sitting along side colorful words come to life in my mind drawing pictures as they pull my thoughts together. But sometimes, even the most telling and detailed sentences are not enough to help me comprehend what is being said to me.

For the first several years of our marriage, Tom had no idea I was misconstruing his thoughts because, from his perspective, he had been clear and articulate. He was left to think I had just failed to listen to him while I was left wondering why he did not care that he had confused me so. My friends tell me their conversations with their spouse can also become confused and exasperating, particularly when they are engaged in discussions that require any intellectualizing or philosophizing, maybe something to do with their morals or ethics or religion or their ethereal ideals and values. But our communication discrepancies came more frequently than once in a while. Even when we spun words around the mundane and the routine – movies we had seen, books we had read, chores we had to do and trips we planned to take – even this kind of small talk, anchored in passing a few ideas or a bit of time, could send my thoughts and contemplations into a swirl of disarray.

I cannot adequately describe how convoluted our discussions became, back before we knew each other's style of communicating was wreaking havoc on the messages we were meaning to convey. Suffice to say we would both argue for hours, all the while thinking to ourselves that nothing we were hearing was making any sense. I know that from my perspective it was almost as if my husband would begin to speak a foreign language. I would hear the words that came out of his mouth, but I simply could not attach any meaning to them. It was if they were random words pulled from a dictionary, placed in a sentence and then set before me as a complex and unsolvable word puzzle. I vividly recall many times when I would see my thoughts swirling in a tide, trying desperately to grab onto something familiar and safe. For years I thought this was the way it was for everyone. After all, isn't this what popular culture and the mass media tell us, that men and women are unable to communicate, that they are wired too differently to ever connect? I came to believe our inability to communicate was the norm. I convinced myself every woman felt like each word from their husband's mouth ran backwards, slipped through thresholds and hid under the surface never intending to be found. I even knew, was just positive, that wives across the world reacted like I did when their ears and mind were deceived. I believed each of them fought with their breathing for control of their speaking voice and their consciousness. Yet when I would ask other women if they could relate to my experiences, they would tell me they could barely even understand what I was trying to describe to them, much less relate to me. Of course they had arguments, they would tell me, but not like that. They never felt they were losing sight of the real world or that their husband was speaking in tongues. They simply reported that they and their spouse disagreed on an issue, told one another so, had their discussion and then either went their separate ways or got over the discrepancies. It did not take long for me to realize that once again, I was not following a normal path. Once again, I found myself face to face with my Asperger traits.

Nowadays I try very hard to gauge whether or not my reactions are being manifested by AS or by something more discrete. For instance, if I find myself in the middle of an argument with Tom, I will consciously stop speaking and run the specifics of the conversation through my mind as if it was a computer that could seek, find, and sort out all the extraneous variables that I relate to AS. I then imagine in my thoughts, two stacks of index cards – one that contains commonplace variables like stress and sleep deprivation and hormones, and one that contains AS traits like my rigid thinking or literal mindedness. Piece by piece, I then analyze a few sentences at a time, methodically analyzing which category of variables influenced each verbal exchange. For example, I typically ask myself questions like: could my understanding of this statement have been influenced by my rigid thinking; am I just under too much stress right now to hear anything properly; did I take his comment too literally; or am I misconstruing the implication of his word or words. Once I decide which influences are at play, I can then sift through the exchange again, this time throwing out the pieces that I think my AS has affected. At that point, I can finally reevaluate the conversation and determine where things began to fall off track.

Sometimes, I will be able to fix things up by asking Tom to redefine or elaborate a specific point or I might choose to ignore an entire passage or two deciding it is just too convoluted to sort out, or I might come to the conclusion that my husband himself made a comment that was just plain rude, wrong or misguided. When I have an inkling the crux of my confusion and my inability to follow his thoughts is more influenced by my AS than anything else, I will directly say to Tom – *I think my AS is confusing me. Please start over and tell me again what you are trying to tell me.* This confession of mine has never failed to help both of us stop the arguing immediately, whereupon Tom can begin his point all over again, but this time with a great deal more care and precision behind his words. However, if I come to believe one of the non-AS variables is at play, I will usually do what my friends are able to do, state my argument and go on my way. More often than not, I tend to believe it is my AS that is interfering with the moment.

Most of the time Tom can restructure his conversations until I can decode what he is telling me. On other occasions there is nothing he can do to forestall my rigid thinking – nothing. Typically I am inflexible in my understanding of words that convey time or order or specific action. For instance, if Tom told me he was going to leave his office in a few minutes, run by the bank, stop by the store and then pick me up from the library, I would expect him to do exactly those things, in exactly that order, in exactly that time frame. It would not do at all if he changed his mind and left the office an hour later than he had planned, ran by the bank, came to pick me up and then suggested we run by the store. Something as seemingly innocuous as this will send me over the wall each and every time. I would have been terribly shaken because he did not leave the office when he told me he would, and also because his actions did not follow the sequential order he told me he would follow. Even if I had been enjoying my time in the library and were anxious to get to the store myself, I would still be unable to tolerate this breach in time and sequence. These episodes become lost in my perseverations. Times when I cannot, despite all attempts toward the opposite, let go of a train of thought. It is as if my mind has trapped the contents of everything that has been said or shown me, far beyond the walls of a house of mirrors. When this happens, my husband has learned that the only thing he can do is ride time until I can settle my dizzying thoughts onto something untouched by my panic and my confusion.

I do not feel my rigid thinking would be a big impairment to my ability to communicate if I did, in fact, move on completely. However, I rarely do. I keep breaks like this – changes in routine, misused words, alterations in sequence, times when I have been utterly confused and then angered – in a file that I access and reexamine in total each time I face a new bout with my rigid thinking. Unfortunately, each time I begin perseverations on one particular issue, I am very likely to recant a litany of similar instances and sets of circumstances, even from as far back as a decade or more ago. Thankfully, Tom has a strong threshold for my perseverations and my rigid thinking patterns. I suppose he has finally come to accept that this chink in my character is as much a part of me as are my blue eyes.

As odd as it might sound, one of the kindest things my husband ever said to me was, *'You are so weird'*. Not a typical endearment, but nonetheless, it brought me joy because in those few words I found a sky filled with freedom. From that comment alone, I knew that even though Tom recognized my differences, he was still interested in being with me. This gave me the go ahead to confess, if you will, every single sensory issue that exasperated, overran and confused me. It felt so liberating to tell Tom my fingers felt like they were being torn apart when he interlocked his fingers with mine – that I felt bugs under my skin when he touched me lightly – that my mouth watered and my nose burned and my stomach turned when he wore certain kinds of cologne – or that when he came too near me, it took everything in me to keep from shoving him aside.

He took each admission in stride, simply nodding as I explained what I was feeling when assaulted by certain sensations. Never once did he complain when I exclaimed I had to leave a ball game because the crowd's constant commotion and moving about made me feel lightheaded and disoriented. Not ever did he tell me he was angry or hurt because I refused to sit too closely to him or hug him often enough or display outward affection like other couples do. At no time did he appear embarrassed or chagrined in response to my social blunders. Still, I worry that I am in some way leading him to feel he is missing something in me, a certain tenderness or smoothness, a softness or a kindness… a special something that only he can define, but that I cannot discern for myself or exhibit on my own. As a sort of insurance policy, as protection from the fact that I might not be as affectionate or pliable as he might like, I work at asking him to tell me when and if he needs more from me than he is getting from me. But because I suspect he will never burden me with the notion that I am disappointing him, I have taken it upon myself to try something that so far has managed to help me make small changes in my behavior. Like other people make lists to remind themselves to pick up milk or get the mail, I make lists that tell me how to act. On my list are things like – *hold Tom's hand for five minutes every day; squint eyes when in an overwhelming crowd; say 'Excuse me' instead of 'I have to get out of here now!'; count to five before replying; hug Tom three times today.* When I review my list, I remember how I need to act.

I am convinced I benefit from this strategy, despite its simplicity. It seems to stick things in my memory – rules and skills and planned behaviors that I would never contemplate or remember to do without prodding, but I am routinely surprised that I need to rely on something so contrived. I have an excellent memory for most things and I am tempted to think I should remember to do something the moment I tell myself to do it. I suppose this discrepancy occurs because there is a subtle difference of content at play here. The memories I easily recall are all based on facts I am interested in or situational events that happened in my past. For some reason, I cannot seem to recall how to act as easily as I can recall how I did act. It is as if when I look backwards I see a photo album filled with vivid images and shapes, but when I try to look forward I cannot call to mind one reliable picture to guide me along. Instead, I spend a great deal of time imagining how things should happen, rehearsing possible scenarios over and over, contriving lines I might say, and directing how others should act and how I would react to their reactions. I will play this game until I feel I have exhausted every possible scenario, and then I will typically obsess over which scene is most likely to happen in real life. But, of course, things rarely turn out exactly as I had rehearsed and so I suppose it will never be possible for me to always know how to act. The human saga is just not reliable enough for me to predict.

Social situations are not the only things I find unreliable, and hence, untrustworthy and uncomfortable. My sense of visual perception often plays tricks on me, making it difficult for me to do ordinary tasks like picking an object from a background, seeing discrete differences among similar objects, or judging if things are close or far in proximity to where I am. Generally speaking, I know I should not rely on my own visual perception, but practically speaking, it is sometimes impossible to rely on anyone else. It is embarrassing to admit to people, strangers especially, that I am disoriented, that I cannot pick my car out from others in a crowded parking lot, that I cannot find my way out of a mall or down a series of hallways in an office building, or that I cannot even easily find my way home in my hometown.

When I know I am going to be in a situation that might render me helpless, I try as best I can to prepare solutions to every problem I might face. For example, I might ask my husband to draw me a very elaborated map pointing me where I need to go with both written and visual cues to assist me. Then we go over the directions verbally until he feels certain I will not lose my way. Finally he hands me the portable cell phone with firm instructions to call him the moment I get lost, kind of an inevitable conclusion for me. I prepare, too, for what will happen once I do find my way to my destination. I try to park my car next to a big visual landmark, something I can lock in my memory for safekeeping until I need it to direct me to my car. I try also to avoid big malls, opting instead for small, self-contained stores that sell everything I need under one roof. I will also talk to myself as I am navigating my way through buildings or down streets, reminding myself to calm down, make mental notes of what I am seeing, have confidence and keep in mind I can always stop and call home for help.

I never feel silly or stupid calling home for help. If I did, I would never do it. I feel safe knowing I am guided by my family's concern and their capable abilities. I feel less anxious knowing they are in my backfield, especially when I come to the terrible realization that I am hopelessly lost. I hate getting lost. I hate seeing the world as a distorted nightmare made up of secret passageways, false exits and trap doors. I overreact with panic. Beads of sweat pale my face, the back of my neck and the palms of my fingers feel clammy and numb, a fast pulse pushes my blood through my veins, my shoulders tense, my mouth waters and my stomach pumps acid to the back of my throat. Yes, it is a natural response to fear; yes, it is a natural response to anxiety, but it is also something more to me. My panic attacks are often very real warning signs, very real unspoken voices that shout to my sensibilities – *Be careful, look around and take note of the surroundings, for you are now in real, tangible trouble.*

I recall one time when Tom and I were in San Francisco on a business trip. His days were filled with work and mine were completely free. After my first day in the hotel room, I decided to take our rental car to a teddy bear factory in hopes of designing my daughters a homemade teddy. I walked into the room where Tom was conducting business, completely interrupting his work, and blurted out that I needed the keys to the car. I remember him looking as if someone had just put a bright light in his eyes, so surprised and concerned was he by both my behavior and my request. Having been caught totally off-guard, he gave me the keys and just sat there unable to speak. As soon as he did, I noticed I had become the center of attention, and quickly concluded I had stepped on yet another social morality. I could not have gotten out of that room fast enough, so embarrassed was I. I grabbed the keys and ran to the garage where our car was parked, finally found it after much delay, and set out toward the factory with only the hotel city map to guide me.

Within five minutes, I knew I had made a dreadful mistake. I compared the street signs I was passing to those listed on the map and found no matches. I decided to stop at a gas station and ask for directions on how to return to my hotel, thankful its address was printed on the map. I crossed traffic to the first place I found and got out of the car to do just that. Within moments a homeless man ran to me, threw himself at me and asked me for money. All at once, I was both frightened for the man and because of him. My heart broke for his predicament, but my body shook because of mine. I was not certain what he or any of the other people I suddenly noticed standing around me would do or want of me, yet somehow I managed to politely tell him the truth – that I did not have any cash. Growing ever more confused, I turned to see the gas station attendant was safely locked behind a set of steel bars. Looking around some more, I was able to determine that I had wandered into a part of town that would not have been considered safe under any circumstances. I stood there paralyzed with the fear that comes when I am lost, the fear that tells me when my safety is in jeopardy. Not knowing where to go from here, I backed away from the onlooking crowd and began to fumble with my car keys. The more I fumbled, the more confused I became. In my confusion, I failed to notice that an extremely large man was standing near me. I have no idea where he came from or how he came to be by my side without my realizing it, but the moment I did see him, I knew he meant me no harm. To begin with, he looked as out of place to the area as I did. He was very well dressed and driving an expensive car. His voice was clear and calming and articulate. He smiled and quietly asked me if I could use some help. Though he did not invade my private space, he was close enough to me to invade the space of the street people who were making their way to me, making it clear by his presence that they needed to move on and away from me. Like a wave that was beginning to recede, I found my pulse return to normal. I rambled on about being lost and frustrated and how sad it was for the street people to live in such deplorable conditions and on and on and on. I knew my words were coming out on top of each other and I knew my conversation was drawing attention from my main problem, but still I rambled. The man listened intently until I found the wherewithal to close my mouth and focus my mind on the reality of my situation. I was lost and had no idea how to find my way home. Very softly, the man told me how to return to the hotel by using specific landmarks and cross streets. He then helped me to my car, shut my door and stood by me until I was safely on my way. Of course, I never saw him again, except in the dream I still have that takes me back to that time and place; the dream that forces me to accept my perceptual disability for what it is – a disability that can lead me beyond my limits.

It took me over an hour to find my way back to the hotel, but I did get home safely. A frenzied and frantically worried Tom met me in our room and repeatedly told me I could never, ever, do that again. I promised him I would never go far without him in a strange place again. And I meant it.

Slowly, at a snail's pace, I am learning to question my actions before I make them. This does not mean I will not continue to make mistakes in judgement, even mistakes that bring me precariously close to danger. What it means is that I am progressing to the understanding that it is in my best interest to use the faith I have in Tom as my insurance policy. In other words, I am learning to ask him if it is a wise decision for me to jog in an unfamiliar park, or ride my bike alone through any given area, or take a short drive to a city I may or may not be familiar with. I know to ask him about the safety and wisdom behind any action that moves me beyond my routine. Like a seeing eye dog, he leads me to safety each time I let him.

After my parents had done all they could to push me along, Tom came just in time to drag me, sometimes screaming and kicking, to a place where I could find real comfort. With Tom's help I have been able to move along the autistic spectrum from the childhood I can barely believe was mine to the relative ordinary I find these days. And as a testimony to his goodness for me, he has never given me more than a nod or a smile to tell me how I am doing. He keeps me safe. He reins me in. He lets me know if I am wandering too far in my thoughts or carrying on too long with my dialogue. I can look at him and see from his expression how my conversation is going and how my audience is taking me. And never do I come to feel he is acting possessively or egotistically or because he is annoyed or upset with me. Even when I only have a slight grip on the reality of his influence over me, I can tell he is trying to teach me and guide me, not keep himself from embarrassment or myself from shame. Because I always knew he was a very confident man who let no one's perception of him tie him down, I knew, too, that he would never let how others saw me, affect him, or us, in any way.

He never missed a beat when he discovered I was different. He never discusses it unless I bring it up. He never alludes to it during my long-winded monologues. He never uses it as a sword to kill my enthusiasm for our relationship. And because he never uses who I am against me, I came to trust him.

Trust. An illusive concept, one so dependent on the ability to generalize, so tied to an ability to read the subtle nature of the human condition – no wonder it so often falls beyond the AS person's world of discovery. But, when it is found, it becomes a life preserver, a means not toward an end, but an awakening. With someone I trust implicitly by my side, I know I will continue to grow and progress, to seek and to find.

Sometimes all I need to keep from falling over the edge is to look at Tom's face. I am stunned by the looks of his face, not so much because he is an attractive man, but more because, in the structure of his face, I see so many of the visual elements that appeal to me – linear lines, symmetry, straightness, perfect alignments. His face is firm and anchored and definite. It is chiseled and solidly cast. It is a visual respite for me. I am oddly calmed when I look at his features, so calmed that I find just seeing him puts me at ease, just as looking at a peaceful stream comforts others and a lullaby soothes a baby.

I often wonder what course my life would have taken if I had met Tom back when I was a teenager twisting and turning my way through youth. I am tempted to think he would have saved me from the turmoil I swirled in; tempted, not convinced. I think it was best we met later on in life, because it took me years of self-study to recognize who I was and how I worked and what I needed to fix me up. Had Tom, or anyone else for that matter, caught me each time I fell, I worry that I would never have been able to figure out what made me tick. I needed to fall, scrape my knees, knot my heart, and try my very hardest before I could really see that I was more than simply a bit different. I needed to come face to face with all of my issues before I could admit I needed the support I now get from Tom. As I go on to lose more and more of my AS, I caution myself never to overburden him with my needs, to never fall in on him, to lean on him only when I am faced with those things that toss me in circles and make me take unusual turns. And as I continue to refine how and when Tom can help me, I try desperately hard to give him the kinds of things I can, things like loyalty and honesty and reliability and shared interests. Like bookends, we have learned to support each other when the stuff in the middle pushes us apart.

6

Rocking My Babies

Oh My God!

A one act, one scene play based on a true story.

The setting: *The hospital ultrasound laboratory.*

The characters: *an ultrasound technician, a nurse, an Asperger Mom-to-be and the nervous Father-to-be.*

The plot: *Things are not progressing as they should be during what should have been a normal pregnancy and the primary care obstetrician is concerned for the baby's safety. An ultrasound is ordered and is just beginning...*

The technician: *Here we go. This might be a bit cold (pours lubricating jell on the Mom-to-be's stomach and begins using the ultrasound wand). Alrighty, I can see what I need to now. Here's one head... (takes a pause and a deep breath) and here's the other head.*

The Mom-to-be: *Two heads? You see two heads? The baby has two heads? (Mom-to-be gasps and with horror in her eyes, looks over at nervous husband who is beginning to slide to the floor).*

The technician: *Dad? Dad are you all right? Looks like we lost another one. (Shouting to the outer office) I need help in here, we've got another dad on the floor.*

ENTER the nurse who begins to tend to the nervous husband, helping him to sit up, catch his breath, etc.

*The Mom-to-be: Oh my God! I can't believe my baby has two heads.
(She begins to shake uncontrollably.)*

The technician: *Two heads? Heavens no. Didn't you know you were
having twins?*

The Mom-to-be: *Twins? Oh my God!*

THE END

They say truth is more unbelievable than fiction and if my life is
any indication, I would have to say, I agree. It is true that when the
short scene above played before me in real life, I truly did think
my baby had two heads. While I am not certain this illustrates the
literal mindedness that often grabs hold of my AS, I do know it
sets a perfect stage for my life as an AS parent. For the past twelve
years, I have felt as if I live in a topsy-turvy world of bemused
consciousness, somewhere in between what should be and what
is. In our home, for example, my children provide me with just
about as much role modeling as I provide them. While I am able
to set forth the more mature hierarchy of moral and ethical
standards, the kids are able to show me how I should act and
behave in public. In fact, they often lead me through public arenas
knowing that without their help, I am likely to both literally and
figuratively lose my way. The kids force me, by their very
existence, into a realm of reality that before their arrival was
hardly of any matter to me. Because I deeply care that they are
well cared for – well educated, happily engaged, and in all other
ways, satisfied young beings – I try as hard as I can to control and
monitor my behaviors and thoughts consistently. I try to be Every
Mom.

While parenting brings out the most normal in me, it also
showcases that about me which is the most unconventional and at
times unacceptably challenging. As it is with most things, I find I
cannot point to one or two of my challenges as an Asperger mom
and shout – *'Ahh, I am a failure!'* No, it takes more than one fall to

trip me up completely. It is in the sum total of my confused state of parenting awareness that gives me reason to quietly whisper – *'Oops, I think I have made a mess of things, again!'*

It has been my experience that each stage of my daughters' lives is not only new to me, but foreign as well. Just when I think I have mastered one set of demands and expectations, another surfaces and throws me off balance. I realize I am not alone in this thought. Every parent I have ever spoken to confesses to a shared set of common complaints, confusions and mistakes. What intrigues me is their identification with the situations and difficulties they discuss. The parents I know seem to have the same kinds of experiences to recount and the same kinds of problems to relate. My worries and blunders come from places they do not seem to know exist. My issues are as foreign to them as their issues are to me. This used to bother me tremendously. It used to make me feel I was incapable of being an acceptable mom. Now that I know more about AS, I am not so hard on myself. I am not so critical. Finally, I can talk to other parents about their thoughts on parenting and discover, if not many, then at least one similarity: we are all able to understand it is possible to adore our children without adoring everything that goes hand in hand with childhood.

I was glad to hear other parents admit their tummies turned over and their ears hurt when their baby came home from the hospital. It made my problems with baby overload seem a little bit more normal. A little bit, not a lot. When I spoke to new parents it was obvious they were terribly bothered by the thing that challenged their sensory system, but only while it was in the middle of its challenge. They were able to tell stories of extra stinky days or extra loud middle of the nights, but none of their stories were filled with the kinds of strong emotional reactions mine were. They would tell me something like, *'There is sure nothing worse than a bad diaper'* or *'It really drove me nuts listening to my child scream all night.'* And that was that. When I asked them to elaborate, to tell me what it did to their system, they would tell

me, *'Oh it bothered me all right. Really made me nervous.'* I would sit
and wait to hear more, to hear something that would have been
more familiar to my own experiences, something that went way
beyond words like bothered and nervous. I never did. It occurred
to me that my experiences might be over the top for
neurologically typical parents.

Virtually everything about new parenting had the potential to
knock my sensory system out of control. Even the most simple
and refined events could prove to be an ambitious opponent
fighting to win my calm. When my first child was born, I took a
bit of interest in designing the perfect nursery; trouble was, the
baby stores and I never agreed on what a nursery should look like.
For example, why pastels? Why do colors that look like they are
covered in a fine mist of chalk dust throw themselves over so
many nursery accessories? I find pastels difficult to look at. I tried
them once. I painted my entire home in light colors. Two weeks
later, I repainted everything in clear, deep tones. Each time I walk
into a room filled with washed-out hues, my mouth fills with
saliva and my head hurts. They make me feel icky, queasy, uneven.
I can take them in small doses, in crayon boxes or mixed in a
fabric that is based in a darker color, but I do not like to feel
immersed in them. They drown me.

When I did manage to discover a section of true colored
furnishings and bedding, my troubles were not ended. An array
of different, but no less irksome, problems stood in my way. I
brought my fixation on symmetry with me wherever I went,
always relying on it to set the reliable standard. Baby things
tended to be rotund and round, no doubt because sharp edges can
hurt little hands and bodies. My logic understood and
appreciated the reasoning behind the designs, but my sensibilities
were unaffected by the vision behind the forms. My eyes wanted
to see solid forms crafted from squares and triangles. They did not
want to look upon a string of black and white abstract patterns,
farm animals that looked like they had been flattened by a tractor,
or clowns wearing pastel costumes. I could not imagine that my

baby would want to lie beneath the belly of any of that either. The things were frightening, not comforting; distorted, not cute.

It was just as bothersome trying to find nice bedding, curtains and wall hangings. Once again, I had to face the pastels and endure the convoluted patterns, but now, I had to deal with their textures, as well. All sorts of sensations apprehend me when I touch certain surfaces. I do not like to touch raw wood, though I like to smell it; but then again, I do not like wood that is finished too glassy. I like to touch wood furniture and floors when it feels like the very last sanding was left beneath the varnish. I am pleased with furnishings that could withstand a strong wind, not pieces that look like they will break when I sit in them. I like very finely woven cottons, very bumpy chenille and rough velvet. My fingers withdraw when I touch satin, polyester, nylon, unbleached linen, and hairy yarn. I will not lie under blankets advertised to be as light as air, nor under blankets too heavy to kick off. Mid-weight fabrics with a subtle nub, bring me comfort. Anything else, brings me goose bumps. I was not certain if my babies would share my idiosyncracies with such matters, but I knew that if I was going to handle the materials they touched, I would have to surround them with necessities that appealed to me. When all was said and done, I did manage to decorate my daughters' rooms in a fashion that was warm and welcoming. I never was able to find any bedding, though, and turned to my mother to make draperies and covers from white cotton. It was a relief to know I could go to the nursery with focused energy. It was not a relief to know the rest of my senses would not be so easy to tame.

Motion is not my friend. My stomach tips and spills when I look at a merry-go-round, or drive my car over a hill or around a corner too quickly. When my first baby was born, I soon learned my troubles with vestibular motion went beyond amusement parks and car rides. I could not rock my girls. I could sway, though, and this I did even in my rocking chair. Leaning forward toward the edge or far back into the chair, I would move my body left and right while I patted the babies to quiet their tears. When that made me sick, I would stand and sway, only a few inches in either direction. If that proved to be too much, I walked the floors, bouncing my daughters up and down as I went. My attempts routinely fell short of perfect for my young ones who preferred the wild ride their father could provide them. Too bad that excuse did little to convince him he should take all the night shift duties from me.

Each time I made any decision to do anything with my babies, I faced the possibility of sensory overload, especially if any smells were involved. Nothing, not colic that woke the neighbors, midnight trips to the store for diapers or all night feedings, could compete with baby spittle, soured formula, cradle cap crust and nasty diapers. The best parent has to hate those things, but I suspect I may have been more affected than most. I would pale, throw up and have to lay down when the odors were too rank.

Surprisingly, I was pretty tolerant of my babies' noises. I did not like the crying and toy clanging, but I could tolerate it. I wonder if this was because I was more focused on the reasons for the cries than I was on the sound of the cry itself. My father always tells me to try and find something to take my mind off my own thoughts and anxieties. He knows me well. The thought that my children were crying because they were seriously ill worked wonders to shove other thoughts, and all other concerns, quickly out of my mind.

There were times when I ended my day worried I had let my children down because I walked out of their room when it was filled with noxious odors or called my husband to rock them for me, but there were never mornings when I did not wake up and tell myself I was doing my best to give my babies the best parts of me. I realized early on, way before I heard the words Asperger's Syndrome, that I reacted to the world in unusual ways, but I never told myself this would mean I could not become a loving and good mother. I was not put together like other moms, but I was still my daughters' mom and I was determined they would have the kind of care they needed from me. I soon learned to put the parenting books away when I came across passages that seemed to suggest there was only one mom, only one way to love a child.

As the girls grew older, new horizons shed a bright light on virtually each of my Asperger traits. And while I could find ways to deal with, or at least mask, my sensory integration dysfunction problems, I could not shirk away from those traits that would follow me no matter what. If we were at home I could do quite a lot to contain my most obvious AS traits. I could control the environment, taking away those things that annoyed me or I could choose to ignore those problems I had not learned to control. At the very least, I could rely on my husband to bail me out if something was happening that would not go away or be ignored. But my husband was not always with me. If I was out on my own when I got too distracted by too many images and situations, I would run the risk of losing my edge over the AS. My language would become too pedantic, my facial expressions too exaggerated, my thinking too rigid, my temper too rude and my pragmatics too problematic.

The situations that caused me the most stress and so the greatest risks, involved my children. I think of my family as a closed entity, one that can invite people to visit on our own terms, when and if we feel up to it. I am easily upset when people do not seem to understand I have a protective shield around my children and my husband. I never interfere with other people's family dynamics, at least not to my knowledge, and I think it only right that I expect others to respect our privacy. My expectations are rarely met and this bothers me. Before we had children, my husband and I were in complete control of our environment. If company came to visit when we were uninterested in entertaining, we would pretend not to be home. If we walked into a restaurant and found it to be too crowded, we would leave. If too many people wanted too much of our time, we quit answering our calls. If the outside world became too invasive, we turned it out and off. We never tried to be rude. We were trying to be honest.

When we had children our privacy vanished. Our closed doors turned to open windows. Our quiet walks down the block became parades all the children in the neighborhood followed. Our phone rang until we picked it up. People knocked on our door and peered in our windows, waving us over to come greet them. I smiled a lot then. I did not know what else to do. I gabbed and laughed and poured lemonade and made cookies and planned elaborate parties for my children and their friends. I was learning the tricks of the trade by reading the neighborhood like a 'how to' book. The only problem was, this book was incomplete. It did much to tell me what to do, but little to tell me what not to do. I could not figure out how not to have children over when the noise was too much for me; how not to speak to neighbors when I had nothing to say; how not to act cheery when I felt closed in on. My emotions were scrambling and my insights were fogged. I knew what I needed to be content but I did not know how to meet those needs without stepping on the needs of my family. I could go back to locking the doors but my children wanted their friends to come play. I could ignore people but this would embarrass my family. I could refuse friendships but this would leave my family lonely. I did not know how to make graceful exits or give subtle hints. I did not know how to make transitions. I did not know how to separate the girls' needs from my own needs without tearing us apart.

Children require a team of people to keep them healthy, educated, happy and socially accepted. This reality did not put me at ease, but it was clear to me and therefore something I told myself I needed to learn to live with. Some members of the team were easier to understand than others. Visits to the doctor's office, for example, were no great mystery to me. The girls' physical needs could be charted, measured, analyzed and fixed. Doctors did not chit chat, they got right to business then moved on to the next person in need. Other fundamentals were not as easy to address or tend to. School issues top the list of those which confound me. The most simple-sounding duties blew me away. For example, what exactly did it mean to plan a child's class party? With no precise guidelines or definition of terms in tow, I had no answer but plenty of questions. Was any kind of entertainment acceptable or did I need to hire a dog and pony act? Could I provide any sort of snack or was I expected to bring in fully nutritious main course meals? Was I suppose to poll the parents and ask them for their thoughts? Was I supposed to invite them to attend? If I planned a craft, were there rules about which materials the kids could use? I did not know where to begin or worse, how to end. The experience was terrifying to me. I was filled with the fear that others would discover my awkward individuality and so I found it very, very difficult to ask others what they did for parties. Everyone else I observed seemed to naturally know what to do, even the new moms. I knew that if I confessed my ignorance or articulated my thoughts, I would run the risk of embarrassing my children. After all, who wanted to be the daughter of the know-nothing mom?

I remember, in particular, one Halloween party when my oldest daughter was in elementary school. My husband and I showed up to watch the party, as did many other parents. We were the first to arrive and sat comfortably in the back of the room, happy to observe. I was content and calm in the classroom; I always am. Young children and the elderly are easy for me to be around. They are gracious toward my differences and accepting, despite my pitfalls. Tom and I talked to the children as they came our way and smiled at the teacher to show we were enjoying ourselves. It was a great party, until the other parents arrived. When other moms and dads came in, it became crystal clear to me that I had missed another unspoken rule. They were all in costumes, we were not. How were they privy to knowledge we did not have? I imagined the worst. Did they have a private club whose members include only those who can recite a secret cookie recipe? Were our names going to be tossed around every

Halloween as the couple who came in street clothes? I obsessed on this worry for days and days on end, until my husband finally convinced me I had made no grand faux pas. But I know I will never forget the feeling that overwhelmed me when my daughter ran to us and asked us why we were not wearing a costume like the other mommies and daddies.

Life goes on for we parents with Asperger's Syndrome traits no matter how many times we ask ourselves what just happened or what could we have done differently. There is no predictability parents can count on, no objectivity that can overshadow the subjectivity innate to children, and no amount of wishing and hoping that can forestall the inevitable... we will make mistakes. The challenge I set for myself is simple. I tell myself I will never know what to do or how to act unless I become a consciously savvy consumer of the parenting market. I have slowly found good friends whom I can ask for advice and guidance, friends who will take me under their wing and never laugh at me or misguide me.

One of my parenting problems is grounded in my inability to generalize information to specific situations. I am only a good problem solver under two circumstances: if there is no real right or wrong answer, for instance when I am writing a creative fiction story; and if there are very clear cut answers, for example the kind that can be found when I design and conduct research studies. When flexible variables affect the situation, things like human emotions, social mores, hidden agendas, and personal biases, I am left without a clue. Most things that involve children seem to include variables I cannot readily identify. Unfortunately, this means I am not a very consistent-minded parent. I approach each new obstacle we come to as if I have never met anything like it before. I end up spending too much time analyzing and rethinking what kinds of reactions I should have to my children's behaviors. I have my rules, but it seems my daughters always find new ways to bend them. Each bend requires me to go back to square one in search of a solution to the problem. I am positive this leaves my children uneasy and, on occasion, undisciplined. They know full well when I will be upset with their behavior; that is never the issue. What they cannot predict, is what I might do about it.

From my long litany of awkward moments in history, one stands out as particularly bizarre, even to my friends who accept my Asperger traits. One afternoon time slipped away from me, leaving me terribly late in picking up my twins from their preschool. I immediately rushed from where I was and what I was doing, and drove myself as fast as I could without breaking the law, to their school. When I got to their building, I ran toward their classroom, right past all the stares and puzzled looks coming my way. I knew it was inappropriate for me to be running down a school hall but I was past the point of worrying about that. I had let my daughters down and I needed to make everything right again. I finally found my twins and was much relieved to see they were calmly talking to their teachers. I gave up my running and slowed my pace to a walk giving the girls time to finish their conversation. The teachers stopped talking the moment they saw me. Their mouths opened, their eyes grew wide and they began to laugh. The girls turned around to see what the laughter was about, but when they saw me they did not even smile. Their little faces looked at me as if they had never seen me before. I could not understand the faces I saw. I did not know why the teachers were laughing and why the girls were stunned. Confused, I asked one of the girls' teachers what was wrong. She broke into loud laughter and said, *'Only you could come here like THAT.'* Puzzled, I looked at one of my twins as she shouted *'Mommy what is wrong with you?'* And then at the other twin who could think of nothing to say. I knew then that I had made another error in judgement. When I flew from the beautician's chair I knew full well I was in the middle of having my hair highlighted and I knew I did not look my best, but I never thought for an instant that anyone would be so shocked to see me like this. I did not think I looked that horrible. I was so surprised to see the reactions around me. To me, my being late had one solution: get the girls as quickly as I could. It did not matter to me if I was covered in red dye or not. It did matter to my daughters. One twin cried all the way home and the other kept finding new ways to tell me how angry she was at me. I did the only thing I can do during times like this. I made an apology and told the girls I hoped they knew I had not meant to upset them.

I worry a lot about the influence I have on my daughters' self-esteem and their happiness. I do not want to fill their lives with anxiety or shame. My concern for them pulls me toward the mainstream even if I bruise along the way. I feel badly I do not encourage them to have many friends over, that I cannot help them with their math homework, that I have to cheat to help them with their spelling. I regret that small talk with the parents of my daughters' friends is not easy for me. I am shamed when I do not know how to act. I do not like myself very much when I hear myself say, *'Be quiet! Stop. Slow down. I can't keep up. Please don't talk to me all at once,'* when my girls are only happily excited to share their day with me. And I hate it each time I realize my daughters have been my teacher more often that I have been theirs.

I know life with an Aspie mom can be very difficult on children. In my case, I can be extremely invasive and obsessive and blunt and loud. I routinely assault my children's quiet and their reflections. I say the wrong thing at the worst time, tell too many stories with too many metaphors too loudly and too fast. I make the most unusual requests and remarks, take things too literally, obsess on the words and actions of others and typically, I am the one who never quite gets the point. I try to reinvent myself, but of course, this is taking time. I find I must settle for the apologies and then something more. I am learning to find ways that explain to them who I am in words they can understand.

Luckily, honesty and forthrightness come with the price of admission for Aspie people. We cannot help but tell people what we think the moment we think it. While this can cause great moments of awkwardness for those we speak to, it really can be a great blessing. I never, for instance, leave my children to wonder what I am thinking. I routinely vocalize my thought process, often to their dismay. Still – ours is a relationship always in the making, always changing and always growing.

I used to hope that I would be able to give my children my best side at all times. I wanted them to look to me as a role model they could rely on, as a mom who showed them which steps to avoid and which way to march. It was never my intention to rely on them as much as I do. Things are often skewed in our family, turned so that the mom ends up relying on the children for their judgement and guidance. I look to them as confidants and best friends. I ask them to help me find my way out of malls, to help me steer my way through a busy crowd, to hold my hand when my anxiety mounts, to tell me if I am saying things no one wants to hear. Amazingly, they never let me down. They take my requests in stride, no differently than if I had asked them to pick up their shoes or do the dishes.

I think the girls must consider me to be a work in progress. I am happy with that because there is so much to be learned from that perspective. If I can show them it is okay to make mistakes and that perfection is not a key to happiness, I will have given them self-acceptance. If I can teach them tenacity and courage in the face of confusion and doubt, I will have given them the will to achieve. If I can show them individuality and freedom of expression are prizes worth fighting for, I will have given them the chance to find themselves. And if, after growing up with me by their side, they learn the importance of acceptance and compassion, then I will have taught them tolerance. If all these things are to be part of who they are, then I will have been a good role model after all. I will have helped them to find goodness in all people and peace in themselves.

These days my family and I are on a well worn path that takes us toward mutual respect and sincere support. Sure we argue and fuss and say things we wish we had not, but then, there is nothing unusual about that. Our relationship with Asperger's Syndrome has not made things between us any more difficult than they might otherwise have been. We allow AS to define us to an extent, but no more than our other genes do. We take it as a given that four of the five of us need glasses and all but one of us has dark hair. We take it as a given that Mom still has struggles with pieces of AS. We know there are many, many things we have yet to discover about each other, and many more things we will learn from each other. Along the way, we are learning not to make excuses about who we are, and we are learning not to wish we were, what we are not. We are learning how to be a tremendously supportive family and sometimes, that is all we need to know.

7

Settling In, But Never Down

On any given day, I can be just like everyone else seems to be.
Until I remember I do not have to be.
The me that I am has finally made friends with the
differences I no longer try to hide.
With effervescence in my heart I now find it easy, natural, right to harvest
what I will and what I need from the places I visit and the people I meet.
And with joy in my soul I am content to hope I have left something
worthwhile, something safe and sound, behind me.

Before she was born, I knew my second twin was going to be a special child. She moved too much, she fussed too much, she never seemed to find calm or quiet like both her sisters had. Sure enough, her birth proved to be difficult. Try as I might, I could not deliver her. Her twin had been born effortlessly, but this baby would not budge. An ultrasound explained why – her birthing position was caught upside down and backwards. The doctors immediately set about the task of moving and manipulating my daughter this way and that, until after nearly twenty minutes, her position was changed to normal and I was able to deliver her without having to have a Cesarean section. I could not wait to see this baby, this child who had fought so hard not to be born. The doctor held her up for me to see, but only for a minuscule moment. *'It's a girl'*, was all I heard. A limp and lifeless baby was all I saw. Within seconds, the nurses took her away to a room I could not see. Everyone left tried to console my fears and abate my questions by showing me the healthy twin, the pink baby who was wailing and fidgeting and sucking her tiny, perfect fist. As happy and overjoyed as I was to see my little first born twin so healthy and strong, as wonderful as she felt in my arms, I could not swallow my fears. I kept asking what was wrong with the other baby, the one I had not met yet. The nurses assured me she just needed a little jump start, a little oxygen and tender loving care. The longest minutes in my life crawled by me until sometime later, how much later I have no recollection of, she was brought to me. Her coloring was not nearly as bright as her twin's. Her movement was slow, her voice quiet. Though they were both nearly identical in their birth weights, this twin looked smaller, more frail, than her sister. My special child was beginning her life in a very special way and all I could do was hold her tight and tell her I loved her.

The doctors never alluded to the notion that she might have suffered any neurological problems, that her development might be delayed, that anything at all would drift from the norm. They never mentioned autistic spectrum disorder. They told us she would be fine. And so it was with much optimism that my husband and I began to raise this child just as we were her twin, just as we had their big sister. Yet there remained a voice in my heart that kept whispering something was different about this child, something…something. Six years later, the whisper became a shout and our world changed forever.

In comparing the twins, it was never obvious to anyone but me that there was any developmental difference between them. But it was tremendously obvious the two had very distinct personalities. Our oldest twin held our hearts with her quiet and cuddling and sweet shyness. Our youngest twin stole our hearts with her energy and her intense desires and her incorrigible tenacity. Life continued for us at a hectic pace as we struggled to enjoy every waking moment with each of our children, maintain two careers, a household, as much of a routine as we could muster, and as much peace and quiet as we could hope for. For the most part, the twins continued to baffle us as all children baffle their parents, and we tried to take every milestone and every missed beat in stride. It was not until the twins began preschool that I would begin to tell those who would listen, something was different about my youngest daughter.

At first, I tried to convince myself my daughter had residual hearing loss as a result of the many ear infections she experienced when she was an infant and toddler. Sharon, our local parent educator, agreed with me, even though everyone else told me I was simply raising a daughter who had her own ideas about what to do and when to listen. They told me my daughter was simply stubborn just like her daddy, or hard-headed just like her mommy. These well meaning opinions never caught my reality. Sharon and I continued to suspect something more and finally, on her recommendation, my husband and I took our daughter to a speech and hearing clinic. As we had suspected, she did have a few measurable developmental delays. Her tests showed she had mild hearing loss and auditory discrimination deficiencies which, coupled together, made it difficult for her to separate one incoming sound from another. Those in the know assured me that though this was not the worst news we could have received, it was news we needed to respond to. We were advised to enroll our child in speech articulation classes and told to have her hearing re-evaluated in a year. And so began the adventure that would take us from insecurity and worry to understanding and hope.

In fast course, I began openly to share my concerns about my daughter's struggles. I stood alone. People continued to dismiss my concerns as nothing more than paranoia and pessimism. Two years of schooling came and went with only me sensing and seeing the subtle differences, the invisible issues that clouded my daughter's thinking. I continued to insist that no matter how normal she appeared, no matter how fine her academic abilities, no matter how on-track much of her development was, my daughter had differences that would sooner, and not later, need attention. I innately and logically knew she was holding on to every ounce of strength she had to keep herself from crossing the line that would take her to total chaos. And yet I had no idea how to help her avoid that deep hollow. It never dawned on me to give her what my father had been able to give me – the kinds of intervention therapies that educators suggest, but that came to him naturally and without a therapist's counsel. To my dismay, I knew I lacked the focus and organization skills of my father, as well as his patience and self-discipline. I knew it would have been impossible for me to do for my little girl, what he had done for me… it would have been impossible for me to help her find her normal without someone else's help. Trouble was, I had no idea where to find her that assistance. Luckily, a friend did.

One evening after a very trying day with my daughter, I found myself talking to a great listener, a friend of mine named Sarah. Forever and ever, I rambled on about the problems my daughter was experiencing, the frustrations I was having at not being able to help her, the confusion I felt from not being able to really identify what my child needed. I explained to Sarah my daughter was often easily upset, that she found it very difficult to calm herself down, that she did not seem to be able to control herself in certain areas like a crowded store or a busy school room or a loud cafeteria. I told how she never seemed to understand my directions, how she refused to wear certain clothes or wash her hair or brush her teeth. I complained that she seemed to be so smart, yet so unable to follow logic or reasoning. I expressed concern over the reality that she had few friends, that she was woefully lacking so many social skills. Sarah listened, nodded and never interrupted me. I knew there was really nothing she could do to help my daughter, but it was a great relief simply to express all of my worries to someone who was willing to listen and not dismiss my words as misplaced ramble. When I had said all I could say, Sarah asked me a question I had never been asked. She asked me if I had ever heard of Asperger's Syndrome.

In no time at all, I gobbled up every speck of information I could find on AS as if it were the very oxygen I needed to breathe. The storm lifted and the answers that explained who my daughter and I were swirled around us like precious gemstones safely washed in with the tide. At last, I had reasons and explanations so rich and real I could almost touch them. Little by little the search I had begun for my daughter's well being exposed my own pattern and structure. Slowly, I let bits and pieces of who I was escape my lips. For the first time I had the confidence to discuss openly how difficult it was to figure out what other people were communicating, how sounds seemed to glue themselves to one another so that it was grueling to pick them apart, how sensory cues seemed bound and determined to overwhelm and, most telling of all, how aggressive our tempers could become and how hard it was to restrain impulsive thoughts and actions. Still, I found most people told me I was just under too much stress or that I had fallen prey to the latest psychological trend, almost saying to me that AS was nothing more than the flavor of the month… a silly fad that would fade as quickly as it had appeared. I was told to relax, to find a real problem to complain about, to accept the fact that my daughter and I were just like everyone else.

I reacted strongly to these kinds of comments, because they implied that my daughter and I were looking for attention and making excuses for our behaviors and our struggles. In not so many words, I was being made to feel that our struggles were like lint we could pick away and toss off, if only we would make the effort to do so. Why, I wondered, did everyone refuse to accept my words as fact and not fiction? Why was I getting so much opposition? Why were my observations being discounted as so unimportant and unreliable? Why?

With Sarah's help, I found the Kansas University Child Development Unit and the answer to my prayers. In a dream come true, I met experts in the field of Asperger's Syndrome who took my comments and concerns seriously. Arrangements were made for my daughter to take a series of tests that would tell us if she was in fact neurologically atypical or 'just like everyone else'. What a relief to know we would have answers, at last.

Time stopped until the two-day evaluation period arrived, though it flew once we began. As I watched my daughter taking her tests, my heart pounded like a race horse running for the finish line. Each of her answers stood like a fine brush dipped in bright colors, eager to paint me a watercolor of who both my daughter and I were. My husband cried as each one of her difficulties became illuminated in her incorrect assumptions and incomplete answers. His heart broke for his daughter, the little one who puzzled him so. Tears streaked my face too, but my heart was not breaking, it was filling up with self-acceptance, it was filling up with possibilities. I knew then, that even though this was not a picture everyone would find beautiful or even acceptable, it was our picture and it was perfect to us. All the insecurities and frustrations I had carried for so many years were beginning to slip away. I had not imagined a thing. I was different. So was my little girl. Different, challenged even, but not bad or unable or incorrect. I understood my husband's tears and his fear for our daughter's future, but I did not relate to them. I knew my innate understanding of what the world of AS is like would help my daughter make her way through life. Together, we would find every answer either of us ever needed.

I had finally reached the end of my race to be normal. And that was exactly what I needed. A finish – an end to the pretending that had kept me running in circles for most of my life. With a heightened sense of assurance, I discovered both my daughter and I needed to answer our own call as best as we could, exactly as we should. I accepted my need to design my own model, one that was built on my strengths and protected, as much as possible, from my weaknesses. It was perfectly okay to be a unique wife, friend and daughter. I could be a quirky mom. All I needed to do was find my way to make things work for the best.

These days, I try to remind myself that though each of my children are very different little beings, I am me and only so capable of flexibility. Within that framework, I then try to give each child what she needs, knowing those needs will often be more than I alone can provide for. In other words, I have learned to accept the fact that I will make mistakes at nearly every turn, but that those mistakes can be softened if I am honest about who I am to my girls. In many ways, it is easier for me to parent my AS child. I know how to relate to her, I know how to show her where to go. I try to teach her to do the kinds of things that help me navigate my way through the regular world. I try to get her to wear earplugs in public or sunglasses in bright light. I try to teach her to very literally bite her lip when she feels she might be about to say something the least bit rude or offensive. Not surprisingly, I have found I am able to rely on a more sophisticated set of learned behaviors than she is able to comprehend at this point in her young seven-year-old life. For instance, I have no difficulty plugging my ears in public or wearing sunglasses indoors and in the evening. I no longer feel odd when I realize my language is yielding to pedantic speech. I openly enjoy talking to myself and never hesitate to do so, even though I now know this is not a particularly acceptable behavior. I will often assert my annoyance in public places, ranting about everything from the loud lights to the sharp sounds to the obtrusive smells and obnoxious behaviors of others. And I have long since given up trying to memorize or understand anything that, by its nature, cannot have a concrete picture attached to its meaning. I no longer apologize when I miss a joke or misplace someone else's convoluted logic. I have gotten used to me. But I am in middle age. What I need to learn to hope for is the thought that I can help my daughter develop the individualized coping skills she will need to find her own comfort zone.

I know now that her answers will be different from mine in large part because she is far more self-aware than I was at her age. I ran about rather carefree in my own world. But then, I had no siblings to compare myself to and no real framework to present myself in front of. I had free rein in how I acted, dressed and behaved. It took me years to care that I was different and only then did I feel the way my young daughter feels now. She is often ashamed and bewildered by the wonder that is her. She is embarrassed the moment she senses she looks or acts differently. Yet though she has the ability oftentimes to sense her differences by comparing herself to others, she is typically unable to suppress her actions or her words and certainly never her thoughts. I walk a fine line when I begin to try to teach my daughter how to act in public, how to understand abstract language, how not to be so outspoken and brash. In one respect, it is very difficult for me because I want her to feel the freedom I did, but without paying the price I did before I came to figure me all out. I never want her to feel ashamed of the qualities that give her the gift of complete honesty. I want her to hold her head up high with an authority that shouts to all who care to listen, *'I don't have to be you!! I don't have to smile when you've done something inane. I don't have to pretend to go along with the flow if it is drowning me. I can choose to turn around and leave this situation the moment it upsets me, and you should respect my decision to do so!'* But then, there is a part of me who knows if she is ever going to find peace with herself completely and if she is ever going to be given the opportunity to succeed in a society as reluctant to accept any deviation from the norm as ours is, I must teach her all I know…and then some.

Life with my Asperger's daughter, challenging as it might be, is something very familiar to me. At any rate, I feel I am parenting the daughter who shares my insights as best I can. The connection we share has bound us together hand in hand. I know far ahead of time if she is going to find a particular environment too overstimulating, a person's style and demeanor annoying, or a comment confusing. As soon as I sense my daughter's thoughts, I look to her and am never surprised to see her looking back at me with a *You see what I see, don't you mom?* expression in her eyes. I feel badly sometimes that she only seems to find that connection with me and not her father or her sisters. They try very hard to understand her uniqueness, but I fully believe there is not much they can do to really 'get' her. To do so, would be impossible for three such normally-placed people. My husband, in particular, struggles to stay one step ahead of her, for that is usually the only way to circumvent her from making a social or problem-solving blunder and more important, a sensory fall. For the most part, we can help her through her misunderstandings of context and her social problems, provided we are there to witness her behavior. We can warn her ahead of time not to say anything about anyone in a voice they can hear. We can prepare her for the place we are taking her to, letting her rehearse in her mind what she will be seeing, touching, smelling, hearing, tasting and doing. So, too, can we encourage her to come to her sisters, one of us, or one of the safe adults we have helped her to identify, should she find herself in a state of confusion or frustration that is too big for her to handle alone. We can ask her to wear her ear plugs or to close her eyes if she is overwhelmed by the patterns she will no doubt find everywhere her eyes wander. We can hand her a flexible ball to squeeze in case she needs to release some nervous energy. We can even tell her some safe topics to talk about and teach her some pat phrases and a few jokes to rely on for conversation. As important as all these skills are, none are as important as the one we cannot really help her with – the skill that will enable her to find her own style and self-identity. She will have to reach that goal on her own. In time, I believe she will.

Little by little, I notice my daughter is trying to find new ways of coping. And what a joy that is to behold. Each time she tries something new, a new technique as it were, to calm herself or to make a friend, it is as if she has won a prize we can all be proud of. Just the other day, for example, while we were shopping at a very sensory intensive store, I smiled with pride as she asked me to put her in a shopping cart and cover her up with everything we were buying. I did so, interested in the outcome, but nonplussed by the request itself. Even her father and sisters, following my lead to allow her this flexibility, continued their shopping without missing a beat. All went well and indeed, she was able to keep her senses from totally dysfunctioning, until we met the check-out employee. The instant she saw my daughter under the fully filled cart, she said in a very aggressive tone, *'She needs to get out of there. NOW!'* My daughter quickly separated herself from the company she had been keeping with the bag of apples, the cartons of milk, the clothing items, the cereal boxes, and dog food and who knows what else. Knowing without even looking at her what was racing through her mind, I turned to the employee ready to speak my thoughts which were quickly coming to a frenzied pitch of anger. Luckily for her, my husband and his quiet demeanor found words before I did, and just as I opened my mouth to scream a stream of indignities at the woman, he told the girls and I to leave the store. His eyes and his hand on my shoulder and his quiet, almost whispered tone, told me he would take care of the situation without causing a scene and further embarrassment for our daughter. Had he not been with us, I am certain I would have let loose one of my biggest Asperger obstacles – my raging temper. We left the store, but I knew some damage had already been done. My AS daughter was devastated. She looked at me with tears in her eyes and hugged me tightly. Her sisters looked on and stood by her as if they too, would join me in any battle to protect her. I stood with my girls knowing we were a team, and for that I was immeasurably proud and glad. But, as I looked down at my frightened and confused child, I knew that without the proper reassurance she would likely never again try to help herself on her terms. I bent down until I was face to face with her, and holding her shoulders as tightly as I could – giving her both deep pressure relief and my total support – I said, *'I am proud of you for finding a way to keep yourself from overloading. You did nothing wrong. You can never be ashamed of trying to help yourself from going overboard. You can cover yourself up with stuff anytime you want.'*

As I asked her if she understood me, it became clear that not only had she taken my words to heart, but that she was also prepared to hand the employee a piece of yet another Asperger's quality she shares with me – her very strong temper. Given a choice, I would rather my daughter stand up and proclaim herself in charge, than I would have her find a corner to disappear in, even if it means having to see her angry – short of violence, of course. Her anger, at least, proves she has not given up on herself and that is no small task. Too often those with AS get lost in a world of discouragement and damaged self-esteem, and in that world there are few avenues for happiness. I try, at every opportunity I am given, to show both my daughter and myself that so long as we are soundly willing, we can find a way to create good things for ourselves – no matter what.

Toward that goal, I routinely tell my daughter she must tell herself it is okay to assess and meet her own needs. I want her to know if she feels the need to lay suspended upside down, or stomp her feet when she walks to feel connected, or squeeze balloons filled with flour, or run to me with whispers of how weird someone appears to her, or seek the company of her dog rather than her friends, or punch a punching bag, even if she feels she needs to shout to keep from disappearing into the abyss so many with autistic spectrum disorders find, then my husband and I let her do so. Our only request as parents who care deeply for her, is that she do nothing to hurt herself or others. Anything within the boundaries of safety, both mental and physical, are boundaries we let her explore, knowing that each is bound to be unique and particularly adaptable to any number of situations.

I know firsthand that my daughter's struggles will not be few, but frequent. But I am very optimistic that she will find her way, just as I have. Beyond the basics, beyond the day-to-day routines, I know the real me, the one that truly matters, was nurtured and shaped by the lessons my mother and father taught me. The heart and soul of their parenting was simply that I take pride in my individuality, idiosyncracies and all. I hold that counsel to be sacred, for what flows from its simple premise is a wellspring of self-confidence, self-assurance, and a dogged commitment to do one's best. These realistic ideals are important to every child's well-being and good health, but perhaps even more so to the child who is growing up while learning to live in a home touched by AS. They are the very lessons I must teach my own children, if I expect them to survive and thrive in an environment shared with me. Why? Because Asperger's Syndrome can mystify those who know nothing about it, particularly in my case when its manifestation has become so subtle. My children cannot point to an obvious physical disability and silently ask others to give their mother a break. Consequently, they cannot expect others to understand me as they do. My girls must learn how to deflect public opinion of their mom, just as they have to look harder to find reasons to be proud of me. I think they have. Within the walls of positive self-esteem, individual fulfillment and goal-setting, I think my girls have learned to accept the public me without too much pain or embarrassment. Sure, they remind me not to talk to myself in public, not to use a loud voice around others, not to bring up the subject of my dogs to every living soul, not to ramble on in my conversations, not to cover my ears at the park and yell *'Who in their right mind can stand all this noise?'* and not to cover my nose and scream *'My God that stinks!'* But that is just fine with me, for all along the way, they never, ever forget to tell me that despite all of my quirks and batty nuances, they love me no matter what.

To be certain my family's love and graciousness toward me never wanes, I tell them as often as I remember that it is perfectly all right and acceptable for them to discover moments when they are unhappy with my behavior, embarrassed by my reactions or even horrified by my conversations. Thankfully, I believe they listen to me when I tell them this, for the last thing I want to do is give them cause to feel badly about themselves should they ever entertain the wish that their mom was more like other moms. I explain to them that every child would like the ability to re-design their parents and I lead them to the understanding that it is perfectly normal to want the fairytale mom. Who wouldn't?

But, along the way, I also try to instill in them a higher moral code, one that is far more vulnerable to decency and goodness. I want my girls to find reasons to enjoy all the people in their lives, even if it means they have to tap into every creative well in their soul, to do so. I want them to truly, way down deep in their hearts, know that all people, and not just their mom, are worthy, viable and exceptional beings who have much to give and even more to share. So long as my family knows who I am, I am rather content. As to others, well, their opinions tend to matter less and less to me. Nonetheless, I do try to help those who need to know me well, see that I simply move to my own music. How I do this, depends on who the person is and on how receptive they are to accepting and acknowledging my differences. If, for example, I am faced with someone who continues to dismiss AS as a passing fad or someone who refuses to believe me when I explain what I really think and feel under certain situations, I separate myself from them as best I can. I have taught myself to believe that if they were my friend, they would not dismiss nor disbelieve me; they would want to know all about me so they could meet me half way. On the other hand, when I sense AS is important to someone, I grow as animated and excited as a returning traveler sharing her fondest memories of a trip well enjoyed. I open my heart and my mind and let everything I know about autistic spectrum disorders fill the silence with both the good and the bad, the challenging and the exciting. I rely on honesty and personal experience and the research of others to guide my talk, never stopping to ask if I am making myself clear, only trying to reveal doors of knowledge that whomever I am speaking to can open when they are ready.

As I look at where I was thirty, twenty, ten, even five years ago, I note how much I have changed, how much I have progressed toward the standard definition of normal. There are times when I approach this fact with a certain amount of excitement and optimism, for I think my history illustrates the myriad of possibilities that can come when the efforts of loyal support systems and friends are combined with a series of proper and early intervention techniques. But I also know that in essence, my AS traits never had a chance to take over my bid for a more mainstreamed life. My IQ is too high, my creativity too productive, my family and friends too supportive for any other option to have emerged.

In some ways I cannot help but be happy I have found a mostly comfortable place to rest. A point in life that sits balanced between neurologically typical and Asperger's Syndrome. In other ways, I meet who I am with a certain amount of sadness, for I often wonder what parts of me I had to leave behind before I came to this place in my life. Would I have been a better writer if I had allowed my skewed take on the world to find its way to paper? Was there a wonderfully quirky and surreal book hidden beneath my idiosyncracies that will now never be found because I can bridle so many of my old habits and thinking patterns? If I had not been taught and encouraged to be as social as I now am, would I have found a different but somehow more satisfying kind of individualized lifestyle? Would I have avoided my irritable bowel syndrome and my panic attacks, if I had not tried so hard to pretend to be normal?

Of course, I will never know. But still I do not want to lose sight of these reflections, because they help me to remember that everyone has the right to figure out their own normal, even as they have the right to know, see and touch how things might be if they work hard to control their differences, if they work hard to modulate, if they work hard to follow the commonplace sense of being. And when all the figuring out and reflecting is finished, the point will remain, that everyone should be afforded a great deal of freedom and respect as they choose who and what we will become.

It can be cozy and warm and right living within the walls of autistic spectrum disorders, particularly those that are as pliable as the AS walls, for there is nothing inherently wrong or undesirable about the need to live alone, to embrace eccentricities and quirks and even blunt speech. There is nothing terrible in having a disdain for certain senses and a craving for others. And there is not one reason why the term *normal* should not be an exceptionally relative idiom. I look at those who wear their AS more obviously than I do with a bit of envy. I admire them their ability to share their brilliant differences. I applaud them for their self-acceptance. I thank them for their realism. And I hope that as we continue to explore the nature of autistic spectrum disorders and the lives that are touched by it, we are able to find much richness and goodness in our common bond. Perhaps then, society will not come to the consensus that those who keep their AS traits intact, either as a conscious choice or because they were never quite able to combine their abilities and exceptionalities any differently, are people who are less than acceptable, less than honorable.

Like other people, those with Asperger's Syndrome are often creative, intelligent, interesting, productive and learned in countless ways. They are often kind, warm, gracious, loving, funny and enjoyable. And like everyone, AS people have their share of hardship, their share of disappointment and dismay. It can be harrowing to see life through surreal lenses that warp and tangle and convolute the most simplest of activities; activities that the neurologically typical consider ordinary, things like shopping and driving and studying and keeping a job and paying bills and visiting with friends. It can be sad to find that no matter how deeply committed the effort, tenuous results may be all that follow. It can be demeaning continuously having to ask strangers for help, friends for support and family for guidance. It can be lonely living in a place so foreign to too many.

Yet, no matter the hardships, I do not wish for a cure to Asperger's Syndrome. What I wish for, is a cure for the common ill that pervades too many lives; the ill that makes people compare themselves to a normal that is measured in terms of perfect and absolute standards, most of which are impossible for anyone to reach. I think it would be far more productive and so much more satisfying to live according to a new set of ideals that are anchored in far more subjective criteria, the fluid and the affective domains of life, the stuff of wonder...curiosity...creativity...

invention… originality. Perhaps then, we will all find peace and joy in one another.

Explaining Who You Are to Those Who Care

Debate rages among those in the Asperger's community whether or not people with AS should tell the world about their challenges and idiosyncrasies. Those who choose to keep their AS private can often find creative ways to work through the social norms and educational systems that surround their lives. But for many, particularly those who are profoundly affected, it might be more effective to educate others about the disorder both in general terms and as it applies to their own situation. Whether or not you make the decision to tell everyone or anyone about your Asperger's is a matter of personal preference. However, the odds are high that there will come a time when at least a small circle of friends, family members, educators and physicians will have to be told, if you are going to receive the advocacy and support you will need to embrace the world comfortably. If the time comes for sharing AS with others, consider the following items as guidelines for discussion.

The potential benefits of sharing

Personally, I believe in full disclosure. I have never hesitated to tell anyone and everyone as much as I know about AS, particularly as it affects my life today. I have convinced myself that people cannot possibly react to me in ways that are valid and real, if they do not first understand the hows and whys of my thinking and acting. For instance, on the surface I am quite sure I can appear edgy, pushy, and much like the prodigal nonconformist, while in reality, down in my heart where it really counts, I try my best to be kind and decent. It is just that sometimes my best is not easily recognized by the outside world. I see my peculiarities as static that interferes with others' ability properly and accurately to tune into what I am trying to communicate. When I tell all I can about that static, I do much to erase its effects, leaving the real me to surface as best it can. I think my telling lets me stand a better chance of making a positive connection with everyone around me, be they strangers in a store or my closest friends and family members.

Specifically, any number of the following reasons might suffice as reason enough to disclose. I rather think there are countless more I have not thought of.

1. You will not have to be as concerned with concealing stiming, ticking, sensitivity to sensory input, social confusion, and other AS traits, when you are around those who know, because you will know they realize those actions are often part of AS behavior and, therefore, nothing to take exception to.

2. Once others have been told about AS, they can become more capable and aware resource and support people.

3. The sooner the general public comes to realize what AS is and how it manifests itself, the sooner AS will meet with broader acceptance and understanding.

4. Perhaps when people know you have AS, they will be more supportive if you choose not to volunteer for certain projects that would be too challenging, for example working as a teacher's aide or speaking on behalf of a group in a public forum.

5. Friends may learn not to expect you to befriend them as they might have otherwise expected.

6. When you explain AS to others, you might help them to identify AS in other people they know who have yet to be diagnosed.

7. Through educating others and sharing the issues of AS, the chances are you will come to really enjoy and appreciate who you are, no matter how different you may be.

The risks involved with sharing

Despite my belief in full disclosure, I will admit there are many times I wish I had never even mentioned the words, 'Asperger's Syndrome'. I have met with some very real prejudices and some very painful misunderstandings on several occasions when I have tried to explain to strangers, friends and even family members, what life with AS is like. I wish I could say I understood their reluctance to be open, empathetic and caring, for if I did, I would find peace. But, I cannot. I fill with anger each time I recall the reactions that have left me cold, frustrated, furious, embarrassed or worse, ashamed of who I am. Still, as an educator, a mother and a person affected by AS, I believe it is best for me to tell people what I can about AS for, in so doing, I hope to dispel the notion that we are in any way less capable or less deserving.

In order to ease the negative consequences that follow disclosure, I have formulated a few coping plans I try to rely on when need be. Simply put, I feel I can react in one of four ways, depending on who I am speaking to and on how deeply I have been upset. For instance, I find that the better I know the person, the easier it is for me to be devastatingly angered by their negative response. In comparison, I expect little empathy from someone who I think has no vested interest in my well being or no real ability to understand the nuances of AS. With those boundaries in mind, I have decided I can (a) relax and be patient in the hope that my sharing of information will eventually elicit respect and sensitivity; (b) put the negative reaction behind me by reminding myself I do not have the power to change the minds of everyone I come into contact with; (c) keep in mind that anger will do nothing but stand in the way of my self awareness and my progress or (d) choose to disassociate myself from the person I am trying to express myself and AS to.

No matter how I choose to deal with the opinions of those I discuss AS with, I try very hard to convince myself that the benefits of sharing are well worth the costs. I tell myself that no matter what happens, I am ultimately in control of how I will react to those who meet my good intentions with their own rude behavior or misguided words.

If you decide to share what you know about AS, be prepared to face the following kinds of scenarios.

1. Because AS is often so very subtle to the casual observer, people may assume there is really nothing inherently challenging, but rather that those involved are simply using the latest psychobabble as a way to make excuses for behavior that might be considered generally unacceptable.

2. Once people learn all that is involved with AS, they may consciously decide to exclude you from their social gatherings, clubs, committees, employment and other group-oriented situations.

3. After sharing the information, people may mistakenly think you are 'just like' those with more mild or more severe neurologically or psychologically based developmental disorders, therefore confusing the issues and not offering the right kinds of treatment, support and expectations.

4. Once you realize others know, you may be tempted to withdraw from society, suddenly feeling too exposed and vulnerable to others' criticism and stares.

Deciding who to tell and how to tell them

When I first discovered the key to my differences could be found in AS, I told virtually everyone I came into contact with as much as I could about AS, as quickly as I could. It was not long before I realized there might be a more satisfactory way of my doing this. Somewhere along the way, I came up with a few different ways to tell different people about my AS, each time depending on the dynamics of our association, how I think they will react to my disclosure and how close our relationship is. Very simply, this generally puts people into one of two groups: those who need to know and those who might not need to know. I never let myself think I will never tell anyone anything. I always keep that option available, in case I need to play it. How you make your distinctions is obviously up to you, but it seems obvious to say that some relationships will depend more on full disclosure than will others. Some in fact, will all but require you to tell at least something about who you are and how AS works with you. If asked, I would define the 'needs to know' and the 'might not need to know' groups as follows:

1. Those who need to know

    (a) People who are in a position of some authority over your actions or future. This group might include your teachers, employers, athletic coaches and even police officers. Without some knowledge of AS, these people will be unlikely to help you meet your needs, but very likely to completely misunderstand your intentions and concerns.

    (b) People with who you are developing a strong, trustworthy and deeply important relationship, perhaps a romantic interest, a very close friend, relatives, roommates or co-workers. These close acquaintances need to know a bit or a great deal about AS, if you expect them to appreciate your differences and be empathetic to your idiosyncrasies and overall lifestyle.

    (c) Individuals you turn to for advice or support, such as your religious leaders, your counselors, your social workers and your physicians. With AS knowledge in hand, these people will better know which kinds of support to offer you.

2. Those who might not need to know

(a) Virtual strangers you turn to only when you have to, such as salespeople, food servers, receptionists, administrators or repair people.

(b) People you come into occasional contact with in classrooms, at work, at the gym, in your neighborhood, etc.

(c) Distant relatives or old friends you rarely keep in contact with.

(d) Your children's teachers, friends, and the parents of their friends.

(e) Strangers you are likely to meet only once, for example people you meet while waiting in line, sitting in a crowded theater or walking on a busy street.

Possible disclosure strategies

Deciding who to tell is sometimes the easiest part of the plan. It is usually more complicated for me to decide how to disclose. Normally, at least one of the following disclosure strategies will prove to be beneficial.

1. Collect and distribute one or two sets of AS research files. In one set of files, collect a variety of reference material that will easily and quickly explain the disorder in layman's terms. Consider using personal accounts and stories, general pamphlets and brochures, video tapes, and your favorite books on the subject. In a second set of files, kept specifically for those who crave or need more knowledge, add academic journal articles, academic textbook titles and research institutions' project reports. (See Appendix VI for a list of helpful resources.)

2. Invite those who need to know about AS to a local or regional meeting or conference on autistic spectrum disorders.

3. Using your favorite form of expression – written, spoken, videos, slides, photography, dance, art, etc.– tell your own story of what AS means in your life, even if you are not the person with the diagnosis.

4. Prepare a business card that contains essential information about the syndrome that you can hand out to strangers whose help you might suddenly need. For example mine reads:

    'I have Asperger's Syndrome, a neurobiological disorder that sometimes makes it difficult for me to speak and act calmly and rationally. If I have given you this card, it probably means I think I am acting in a way that might be disturbing to you. In short, Asperger's Syndrome can make it difficult for me to: speak slowly, refrain from interrupting, control my hand movements and my blinking. It also makes it hard for me to follow your thoughts so that I might misunderstand what you are trying to say or do. It would help me if you would speak calmly and answer any questions I might have, clearly and completely. I apologize if my behaviors seem inappropriate. For more information on Asperger's Syndrome, please write: ASPEN of America, Inc. P.O. Box 2577, Jacksonville, Florida 32203-2577.'

5. Keep AS reference materials visible in your home to entice visitors to read them.

6. Send the names of the people you want to educate to regional and national organizations that provide informative newsletters and or magazines.

7. Devise a list that specifically describes many, if not all, of the things you do which can be attributed to AS. For instance you might list some of the following: I am easily agitated in large crowds; I tend to get too close to people when I talk to them; I like to rub other people's heads; When you frown, I

do not know if you are sad or angry or lonely. Include as many symptoms as you can so that people are not tempted to dismiss your concerns and tell you everyone has those difficulties; the sheer number of your challenges will convince them that you have more issues to deal with than most people do.

Survival Skills for AS College Students

I have heard several speakers at AS conferences say that universities are filled with AS types. With a great big grin on my face, I applaud that sentiment. With a strong support system and a healthy interest in a field of study, those with Asperger's will often find they have just what it takes to make their college years a wonderful experience. Where else but in college can you obsess on your interests and get rewarded for doing so? In what other setting could you create your own sense of style and convention without looking like you missed the point? What other environment would allow you to talk to everyone you see, no one at all, or even yourself, without missing a beat? In other words, where else could you bang your own drum so loudly? No where else that I know.

In truth, going to college is a big step forward for anyone. To be certain it never becomes a giant push backward, you should choose a college that offers a variety of programs and resources designed to meet your special needs. This implies that you will have to tell at least a few people at your college about your AS. Most likely, that list will include most of your professors, a guidance counselor, an administrator who has the power to design your curriculum and course schedules, and possibly someone in your housing unit (unless of course you make the choice to live alone). Use the following list to help you decide which kinds of support systems you might wish to seek when you begin looking for the college/university you think you could attend.

Support systems for social impairment

1. Help improving your social skills

(a) Classes in speech communications, sociology, psychology and dramatic arts programs give those with AS a wonderful opportunity to learn more about social skills, albeit on an academic level. I am convinced I learned most of what I now know about social skills because of the many hours I spent in courses such as Interpersonal Communications, Intrapersonal Communications, Nonverbal Communications, Voice and Articulation, Mass Communications, Oral Interpretation of Literature, Acting, Social Psychology, Child Psychology, Psychology for Special Education, Sociology and General Psychology. Somehow, I was able to dissect the nuances of human behavior far more effectively when I was a student studying it as a science than when I was an individual trying to figure it all out through experience and intuition. If asked, I would recommend AS students enroll in as many of these courses as they can, realizing, however, that it might be wise to enroll in some of them as a listener and not as a student working toward a grade. Some of the courses require a great deal of intrinsic knowledge that if missing because of the AS, would make it hard to master the material in the short time a course typically provides.

(b) Ask your counselor if the university has, or could establish, a friendship group for people with AS and related syndromes.

(c) Ask your counselor to help you find career placement workshops that would teach you how to interview for jobs, write a positive and strong resume, dress in a professional manner and discuss your AS with a future employer.

(d) Try to establish a 'safe' place on campus where you can go to relax and re-group, perhaps something like a corner of a quiet study hall, a remote area of the library, a park bench in a campus garden or a special exhibits room in the university's museum.

2. Help establishing relationships with peers

Everyone with Asperger's Syndrome realizes it can be very difficult to establish close friendships. However, college life affords unique opportunities to make a variety of casual friendships all of which can serve to make the college experience more pleasant and successful. An empathetic college will provide many opportunities for students to meet one another by promoting special interest groups across campus. Ask your guidance counselor to help you find a group made up of people who share your interests or hobbies and then do what you can to make a friend or two from among that group. If your social skills are markedly weak, you might share this information with your counselor who could possibly help you establish a friendship with another student who has volunteered to act as a peer tutor or mentor who would help other students find their way around campus, study, car pool, shop for necessities, find research materials, fill out important registration and information forms, etc.

3. Help establishing relationships with teachers

It will be essential that you take courses only from empathetic instructors who are interested in helping you achieve your greatest potential. These kinds of teachers are often easy to find if you take the time to ask other students who their favorite teachers are. If, however, you feel uncomfortable talking to your peers about this, rely on your counselor to help you identify which teachers would be the most likely to do everything they can to make your time in their classroom productive and comfortable. Specifically, the following items are the kinds of concessions you might ask for, depending of course, on your individual needs:

(a) If personal space or social impairment problems are part of
     your AS, you might ask for special permission to avoid
     group projects, group discussions, partner laboratory
     assignments and group seating arrangements.

(b) If auditory or visual sensitivity is an issue, ask for
     preferential seating away from as many distractions as
     possible (probably somewhere near the center and front of
     the room), copies of your professors' notes and permission
     to tape record lectures.

(c) If literal thinking interferes with your ability to problem
     solve and complete higher level thinking projects, discuss
     this in detail with your teacher who will have to work with
     you and probably your counselor to determine exactly what
     kinds of support and assignments you would most need to
     be successful. Be prepared, however, to be told the class you
     are interested in taking might not be the best for you. For
     example, I know I had a very difficult time in a philosophy
     class, so much that in thinking back, it would have been
     better if I had dropped it or never taken it in the first place.
     Often, colleges will arrange for you to take a substitute class
     (one that was not originally part of your degree plan) if they
     come to believe you really cannot complete the
     requirements of a particular class. This might be your only
     option.

(d) If you have bilateral coordination problems that make
     handwriting difficult, see if your teacher will let you take
     oral examinations, give oral instead of written reports, have
     extended time on exams, use a lap top computer in the
     classroom, and tape record the lectures.

(e) If you suffer anxiety attacks or bouts with depression that
     interfere with your ability to function, you could request
     flexible assignment due dates, flexible testing dates,
     permission to attend other sections of the same course, and

permission to make up missed assignments through extra credit work.

(f) If you are a visual thinker, ask your teacher if it would be possible for him or her to create visual aids for you such as graphs, charts, video tapes, elaborated examples that include a great deal of visual descriptions and computer tutorials that include good visuals.

(g) If you have hyperlexia, dyslexia, poor spelling skills, illegible handwriting or any other reading or writing disability, tell your teachers so they direct you to a tutor or special education center for appropriate support.

(h) If you are easily upset by new routines or quick changes in schedules, ask your teachers to give you at least a few days warning if they are going to have to alter the class schedule, assignment requirements, meeting days or times, or the overall routine.

(i) If you have problems taking turns in conversations or if you interrupt people when they speak, ask your teacher not to require you to engage in group discussions or debates.

Help finding your way around campus

1. Geographic Issues

Many people with AS might find it very difficult to navigate through large college campuses. Like congested shopping malls they can be visually confusing, overly stimulating and stress provoking; all variables that will work against the AS person's academic and emotional stability. The following simple reminders will make sprawling and complicated universities easier to navigate.

(a) **Handicapped parking passes.** The ability to park your car near your building will enable you avoid overcrowded and visually perplexing parking lots.

(b) **Elevator keys.** Ask for these if you find yourself easily disoriented when faced with big crowds and continuous flights of stairs or if you think a few moments in the cocoon like elevator space will help you to calm down.

(c) **Special student transportation assistance.** If the school runs a bus service for students who would otherwise find it hard to drive themselves to campus, inquire to see if you can purchase a pass to use this benefit.

(ii) MAKING THE CAMPUS MAKE SENSE TO YOU

(a) Walk around campus as if you are a photographer and take mental pictures of everything that catches your interest with your mind's eye. Sketch what you see, even if you are not an artist and have to rely on boxes, circles or triangles to represent the buildings, structures, walkways, streets, and landscaping elements you want to include. Use colored pencils or markers to help the sketches look like the real thing.

(b) Write detailed notes that tell you what you will see as you go from one place on campus to another.

(c) Take a tape recorder with you as you walk around campus and record what you are seeing and where you are going. Include all the details you need, but keep separate tapes of each destination's trip so that you do not make things too confusing. For example, record one set of directional instructions that follow your morning class schedule and another that records your afternoon schedule and others that might help you navigate from your home to the library or your home to the athletic stadium or the student center to a shopping mall. In other words, separate each trip as if it were a separate song on a tape.

(d) Practice moving about campus with someone who will help you find your way around. As you do, make certain you talk about what you are doing, and that you do not become distracted by small talk or other discussions. Focus on making a mental, verbal and auditory map. Keep in mind that the more you practice, the better you will be able to imprint the information you need on your long-term memory banks and so, the sooner you will be able to find your way all around campus without relying on your maps or other information.

Making the most of your time and efforts

1. Planning your schedule

Many colleges will make special arrangements with special needs students that will allow for great flexibility in scheduling and graduation requirements. For example, you might be allowed to take less than the standard course load, you might be granted waivers or course substitutions, and you might even be able to plan a completely unique field of study that is designed solely for you. With those thoughts in mind, consider the following things:

(a) Never let an advisor or friend talk you into taking a course that you know will be more than you can handle at the time.

(b) Never sign up for a class that meets earlier than you routinely like to wake up or later than you routinely like to relax. If you are a morning person, do not take evening classes and vice versa.

(c) Try very hard not to take advanced level courses before you have taken their prerequisite courses, unless you have spoken to the instructor and have been reassured that you can master the material without the introductory level course.

(d) Build in time for fun and recreation, no matter how you define those concepts.

(e) Keep drop dates on your calender so that if you decide a course is too difficult for you, you can drop it without affecting your grade point average.

(f) The moment your instructor tells you when homework is due or when tests will be administered, write them on your calendar so that you cannot fail to remember them.

(g) Send a copy of your course syllabi and your schedule to your parents or support friend so that they can help remind you of important dates and commitments.

(h) Do not schedule your classes back to back unless they are in the same building. It can be too taxing to try and navigate your way through campus under time pressures.

2. Study skills

(a) Study your least favorite subject first.

(b) Study during your most productive part of the day, avoiding times when you typically feel tired, restless, hungry, over-stimulated, anxious, etc.

(c) Experiment with studying in the same place – a 'study spot' reserved only for studying, not sleeping, socializing or relaxing.

(d) Prepare short study tools that you can rely on and review when you find you have a few minutes to spare.

(e) Experiment with your environment when you study. Determine if you need quiet or background noise, bright or diffused light, a well organized or messy desk and possibly a snack or something to drink.

(f) Set short-term and long-term goals that you try to meet by a certain time. For example, a short-term goal might be that you set a goal of studying one hour a day for each course, while a long-term goal might be that you review your materials for at least two hours before each examination.

(g) Monitor your attention span, so that if you feel you are growing restless, tired or bored, stop studying and do something else until you find you can go back to studying. Discover how long you can study at one given time and try not to go beyond that time limit before you do change your activities.

(h) Write your notes in a way that sparks your memory most. You might underline or circle thoughts and words, draw arrows or stars by specific concepts, indent major ideas or details, change the style of your writing from cursive to print within each page of notes, etc.

(i) Make use of note taking and study tools

- 3x5 note cards that have short ideas written on them that might include mathematical and scientific formulas, definitions of terms, and general concepts

- an audio tape recorder to tape lectures

- a separate notebook for each class that allows you to keep all your notes, hand-outs, and homework assignments in one place

- a variety of differently colored pens and pencils that will enable you to prepare visually appealing and effective notes.

Help dealing with typical college stress

1. Practice stress reduction programs, which might include yoga or other similar physical exercises, deep breathing, bio-rhythm feedback or meditating. If you do not already

have a program you regularly rely on, ask your counselor to help you find a program that matches your needs and your interests.

2. Turn to your favorite hobby or interest when you feel yourself getting overwhelmed.

3. Listen to the type of music that will calm your nerves.

4. Keep a journal or written record of your thoughts, including your dreams and ambitions, your day-to-day routines, things that make you happy and sad, anything that confuses or frustrates you, and anything that causes you stress or over-stimulates you. Keep in mind there is no right or wrong way to journal. Anything goes. I usually purchase a composition notebook or some other kind of book filled with blank paper and literally put a pen or pencil to the paper until my thoughts flow, even if this means I simply doodle and draw. Words often come after such simple exercises. In a journal, you can write whatever you feel like writing, not stopping to worry about spelling or grammatical correctness, focusing instead on your thoughts, ideas and emotions. If all is going well, your journal will be a great reference for you to enjoy just as you might enjoy a scrap book or photo album. But, if all is not going well, then your journal can serve as a record of when and possibly why things began to get difficult for you. If this happens, share as much of your journal as you can with a counselor, advisor or other support person so they can help you decide how to deal with the issues that plague or annoy you. This would be especially important if you ever come to conclude the stress is beginning to interfere with your ability to stay awake, sleep, eat, take care of your personal hygiene, study, make conversations or simply enjoy life. Stress can be crippling. Do what you can to control it before it controls you.

Employment Options and Responsibilities

I remember my first adult job interview. I had just finished my masters degree program and was interviewing for a job as a career consultant. During the interview, the owner of the firm asked me if I had much interest in the multi-media wave that was on the brink of bringing us hand-held camcorders, video recorders and compact discs. I shared my enthusiasm for the technology, certain I was making great progress with the boss. All went well until the man told me his favorite multi-media company. Rather than telling him I disagreed with his conclusion, or better yet, keeping my mouth shut, I literally put my index finger in my mouth, made a choking sound and screeched, 'Gag me!'. Suffice to say the interview ground to a halt.

Surprisingly enough, I was offered a job, but not as the high powered career manager my resume said I was over qualified for. I ended up working in a tightly cramped room with a dozen other women who spent their nine to five day sitting around a community desk working to assign otherwise unemployed people to temporary jobs. I lasted less than three months. How ironic that I would have thought I could be a career counselor when, in fact, it was I who needed career counseling. In fact, if there is one piece of career advice I would strongly recommend AS people follow, it would be that they find a professional, or at least a very knowledgeable friend, to help them chart their career future as soon as they are mature enough to give credible thought to the matter. To get everyone started along those lines, I have put together the following set of ideas that should serve to stimulate some creative thoughts and viable options.

Career choices: Self awareness and understanding

Before you can begin to decide which career path to follow, it is essential you discover the areas you are most interested, competent and comfortable in. Use the following list to help you make that discovery.

1. Make a list of all the things you enjoy studying, talking about and actually doing.

2. Make a list of your skills and abilities.

3. Explore the possibility of turning one of those interests in to a career. For instance, let's say you enjoy sports. Brainstorm all the jobs that have anything to do with athletics. For starters, you might think about working as a team physical fitness trainer; a sports equipment manager; a journalist who covers games and players, or the history and philosophy of the sport; a sports memorabilia collector and trader; a ticket salesperson; a team's physical therapist; a coach's assistant; a grounds keeper; a sporting arena or field designer; or even an athlete.

4. Research your career options as fully as possible and determine if your skills and abilities are compatible with those mandated by the job. Among the factors to consider:

    (a) The sensory elements of the job's physical environment that involve issues such as the noise level; the lights and overall design of the building, office and/or outdoor grounds you will have to visit; and even the smells that you might encounter. In other words, is the area too loud, busy, crowded, confusing, overwhelming or visually disturbing to you? If so, will this interfere with your ability to do your best work?

    (b) The interpersonal expectations. For example, will you be expected to interact with other employees on group assignments and attend frequent group meetings or will you be allowed to work virtually on your own?

Will you need to talk before large groups of people? Will you be expected to write many reports and/or participate in peer reviews and evaluations? Will you need to attend social functions with the employees? In short, will you be allowed much anonymity or will you need to work with others frequently? If you do have to work with others on a regular basis, will you be able to do so effectively?

(c) The schedule and expectations of the job that might include abrupt changes in routine, changes in the times and days you are expected to be at work, rearranged or even canceled vacations and break times, the reassigning of supervisors and co-workers, new job skill requirements, moving to new offices, traveling to other offices, etc. In short, can you handle a flexible job or would you prefer a more consistent and predictable work environment?

(d) The schooling and on the job training necessary for advancement. Ask yourself if you are prepared, able and willing to attend continuing education classes and seminars that might be required of you.

Finding your dream job

1. Interview skills

This is a tricky skill no matter how you look at it. Two keys to success, however, are advanced preparation and practice. If you take time to do both, you should find the interview process less intimidating and far more productive.

(a) **Role play.** Ask others to help you brainstorm a list of potential questions and concerns your prospective employer might discuss with you. Rehearse what you might say in a variety of situations.

(b) **Non-verbal communication strategies.** Make a list of the behaviors you should and should not do. Go over the list several times a day before the interview is to take place, until you are confident you will present your best behaviors. Potential items to include:

- use an appropriate greeting and goodbye
- use the appropriate vocal rhythms and pitch
- use good eye contact
- try to look calm and happy
- pay close attention to what is being said to you
- sit upright in your chair
- show enthusiasm
- wear clean, ironed and neatly matched clothing
- bathe, wash hair and brush your teeth
- avoid shifting your eyes and gaze around the room
- avoid making extraneous vocalizations
- avoid talking out of turn
- avoid using too many hand gestures
- avoid biting your nails, tapping your fingers or feet, etc.
- avoid laughing at the inappropriate time.

2. Possible career choices

Many people with AS find they are the most successful in careers that do not require them to deal with many human emotions and strong social skill expectations. That being the case, the following careers come to mind.

- writer
- animal trainer
- engineer
- computer programmer

- horticulturist
- university instructor in the field you most enjoy
- research analyst
- artist or craftsman
- musician
- assembly line factory worker
- architect
- police or security officer
- fire safety officer
- scientist
- electronic, auto, television, etc. repair person
- carpenter
- librarian
- historian
- antique or special items collector and trader
- and anything else that captures your interest, builds on your strengths and affords you the kind of environment you need.

Making your job a success

1. Special accommodation requests

Whether or not you decide to tell your employer and/or your fellow employees about your AS, you might ask if you can rely on any of the following services or accommodations which might help you to control the AS traits that could interfere with your job performance. And keep in mind it is important for the employer to realize you are not asking for special compensations that will release you from work responsibilities, but rather special concessions that will help you to do your absolute best work for the company.

(a) ear plugs or stereo headset

(b) sun glasses

(c) word processors

(d) calculators

(e) an office or work space in the most quiet place possible

(f) advanced knowledge of any changes in routine as soon as possible

(g) a mentor or co-worker you can train with or work along side of

(h) a flexible break schedule should you need to quickly find a quiet zone

(i) assistance in filling out your employment forms and contracts

(j) a regular parking space close to the building you will be working in

(k) the opportunity to request which people you work with on group assignments

(l) continued career and job skill training.

2. *Your responsibilities*

(a) Never assume your employer or co-worker should accept anything less than your best efforts. In other words, always do your best.

(b) Always let your employer know if you cannot make it to work or if you will be late or leave early. It is not fair simply to assume that co-workers will cover for you without your having made the effort to explain your absence.

(c) Never underestimate your own potential.

(d) Do everything you can to improve your skills or widen your knowledge.

(e) Try to be patient with people who seem to ignore your needs, they might simply need time to adjust to your differences or more education in order really to understand the AS world.

(f) Try very hard to find employment that holds your interest. If you do, you will be far more likely to control any of the AS behaviors that might otherwise make it difficult for you to do your job.

(g) Try not to quit a job without first giving at least two weeks notice. This implies you will be honest with yourself about how the job is going, so that you can judge whether or not you are beginning to feel overwhelmed, overloaded or too frustrated by the demands. The moment you feel any of these sensations, you need to talk to your employer or mentor and either find a way to deal with the situation or prepare to leave the job.

(h) Tell your employer and co-workers what you think they need to know about your AS, if you decide that this will help them to better accommodate you, understand you, and help you to find the kind of work you are best suited for.

(i) Let your employer and co-workers know you appreciate their friendships and their guidance by sending them a thank you note once or twice a year or by simply telling them how you feel about their association with you.

Organizing Your Home Life

I like household routines as much as I like professional sumo wrestling – which is to say I do not like them in the least. I used to feel a tug of guilt when I allowed myself to admit I did not enjoy all that comes with caring for my family and home, but that was before I came to view homemaking as a quasi-academic major worthy of a stack of certifications and degrees. Those who tell you homemaking is easy or that it is enticing only to simpletons, are woefully misinformed. In my view, homemaking is a science that has to be studied, researched, analyzed, learned and memorized. Not because it requires a great deal of intellect, rather because it requires a well-organized and deliberately attentive mind. A mind that can shuffle, sort, file, retrieve, and re-route with only a moment's notice.

I, like many of my AS friends, do not have a mind like that. My mind wanders about like a golden retriever let loose near several reed-lined ponds and an open field, knee high in native grass and wildlife. I never know quite what I am looking for, exactly what needs my attention first, precisely where I want to go, or how I want to approach that which lies before me. I marvel at those I know who are able to handle their home with any measure of efficiency or ease. To me, homemaking is an intricate blend of peculiar demands, random fundamentals, chaotic compromises and irksome annoyances; it is a skilled trade I have no plans of mastering. Still, it is something I try to train myself to do with at least a certain measure of proficiency and a degree of resignation that I would not have been able to offer just ten years ago. After much trial and error, here are the lessons I have managed to learn about homemaking with AS.

Color coding: A foolproof way of keeping everyone and most everything organized

1. The people

Assign each member of the family a color, then try to purchase as many personal items as you can in those colors letting everyone know their things are the blue or yellow or pink or whatever color they have selected. Items you might be able to include in this system include: toothbrushes, hairbrushes, laundry baskets, bedding supplies, towels and wash cloths, various school supplies, key rings, glass cases, lunch boxes, gloves and hats, backpacks and briefcases and toy boxes. Continue the theme by purchasing colored pens and note paper that match each person's color, a note on blue paper is for the person who chose blue, an activity written on the calendar with red ink is an activity for the person who chose red, and so on.

2. Mail

Keep a collection of differently colored bins for the various mail your family receives. One color for bills, one for personal correspondence, one for junk mail you might want to read like shopping ads and coupons, and one for mail you are ready to stamp and mail.

3. Record keeping

Buy different colored filing folders for each main category of information you need to file. Try to select colors that remind you of the category.

(a) **Automobile information** – warranties, the rental or purchase contracts, repair records, and payment books kept in a color-coded file that matches the color of your favorite car.

(b) **Credit card and checkbook records** – credit card information including photocopies of your payment agreements, and the names, addresses and telephone numbers you need should your credit cards or checks get lost or stolen; other general financial contract payment agreements; copies of paid bills and receipts; checkbook information, including your bank account number and the name, addresses and telephone numbers of your bank kept in a color-coded file that matches the color of your favorite currency.

(c) **Family documents** – wills; birth, marriage, baptism and death certificates; divorce papers; diplomas and any other personal information numbers or licenses kept in a color-coded file that matches the color of your eyes.

(d) **Financial records** – insurance policy papers; investment papers; the names, telephone numbers and addresses of the people who broker or maintain your accounts kept in a color-coded file that matches the color of your checks or checkbook.

(e) **Health records** – immunization records, hospitalization records, medical procedure records, histories of family illnesses, allergy records and lists of medications you have taken kept in a color coded file that matches the color of the red cross found on most first aid kits.

(f) **Household products information** – warranties, proper care and handling instructions, and authorized service centers kept in a color coded file that matches the color of your refrigerator.

How to avoid shopping centers and other crowded places that typically contribute to sensory overload

1. Catalog shopping

These days, most shopping, including everything from groceries sold in bulk, to memorabilia, art work, hobby supplies and home maintenance items, can be done by mail order. What's more, if you live in an area that does not require sales tax on those items purchased by mail, you can even save money when you catalog shop. If you are not already receiving a variety of catalogs, ask your neighbors and extended family members for their old catalogs. Or you can search the last few pages of most hobby or specific interest magazines (home decorating, garden, automobile repair, etc.) for catalog advertisements and address information.

2. Gifts

Next time you need a gift, consider sending something that requires no out-of-the-home shopping such as a subscription to a magazine, a donation to a special organization made in the recipient's name, tickets to an event, an IOU for some service you can provide them, or an item you were able to find through your catalog shopping.

3. Home delivery services

Many stores will deliver their products to your door, or at least arrange to have them mailed to you, if you simply tell them you have a disability that makes it difficult for you to drive, face crowds or leave the home. If it is difficult for you to ask the store personnel for this assistance, write a letter instead asking if they can provide this service.

4. Take turns shopping with a friend

Work out a partnership with a friend to take turns doing each other's errands. Or if you find you are better able to function at one store than another, ask the friend if you could take care of the general shopping needs at the location you are most comfortable visiting, while the friend faces the crowds at the stores you need to avoid.

5. Personal shopper

If nothing else, you can always try to arrange for someone to do your shopping for you. If you cannot afford to pay someone, perhaps you could barter a good or service instead. You might offer help with homework to a high school student, a homemade craft you are particularly good at creating, help on tax forms, gardening services or any other number of services you enjoy and do well, in exchange for weekly grocery shopping or small errand running.

Making your way through the day without stressing yourself out

1. Divide and conquer

Make a list of assignments: Write down everything you think you need to do to keep your household running. Include all kinds of responsibilities such as: cleaning, gardening, auto care and repair, volunteer commitments, shopping, and any other activity you will need to engage in on a regular basis – things like getting your hair cut or visiting the doctor. Then, assign each activity a specific day of the week. Keep track of your schedule by writing everything on a large monthly or yearly wall calendar, or in a notebook you have designated for home-making routines. Record the weekly items first. For example, you might decide to grocery shop on Mondays, vacuum on Tuesdays, wash clothes on Wednesdays, dust on Thursdays and care for the yard on Fridays. Then go back and assign a time for your monthly routines such as, for example: hair and doctor appointments on the first Monday of every month and car maintenance on the last Friday of every month.

2. Visual reminders

Get in the habit of carrying small note papers with you where ever you go. Write yourself reminders on the paper that you can tape to spots you are certain not to miss. You might keep reminders of the day's schedule changes posted on your bathroom mirror; reminders to exercise, eating right, read to the kids, etc., posted near your refrigerator; and reminders of things you wanted to tell your family or friends posted near your computer or the phone.

3. Auditory reminders

Record your thoughts, reminders of things you want to accomplish, and appointment times and dates on a pocket-sized tape recorder you can carry with you where ever you go. Listen to it several times during the day to keep your memory jarred, or write the entire transcript down when you have the time so you can have a visual reminder, as well.

4. Fashion sense reminders

If you find you cannot design a nice looking or comfortable wardrobe without distressing yourself, turn to your favorite clothes catalog for help. Simply cut out pictures of models wearing outfits you think you would like and then either order those clothes from the catalog, or take the photos with you to a store you feel comfortable in and ask a salesclerk to help you find a similar outfit. When you get the clothes home, hang them together in the closet with the picture of the model pinned to one of the pieces, to remind you how the outfit should be put together.

Coping Strategies
for Sensory Perception Problems

Although extended research is needed to explore the relationship between sensory perception problems and Asperger's Syndrome fully, experts in the field have begun to conclude there is a correlation between the two (Attwood, 1998, p.19; Rimland 1990). If you are easily upset or overwhelmed by the everyday kinds of sensory information that exist in your life, for example, if everyday lighting can appear intensely bright, quiet music can sound painfully loud, a whiff of perfume can bring on nausea, or certain food textures and tastes produce a gag reflex, chances are you are affected by sensory perception problems. If that is the case, consider engaging the help of a trained occupational therapist who will assist you in designing a formal sensory integration therapy program. In the meantime, the following suggestions might help you manage some of the more common situations. On a cautionary note, please keep in mind some of these coping strategies can look unusual to the general public. Therefore, it might be in your best interest to use the therapies you select in as private a place as possible. If you cannot find privacy, it would be a good idea to tell your close associates a few things about sensory perception problems and how you try to deal with them, so that they will be able to empathize with you when you do your therapy.

Tactile sensitivity

1. If you dislike being touched, politely ask those around you to warn you before they touch you or ask them not to touch

you at all. If you decide someone can touch you, let them know which you prefer, light or firm pressure.

2. If even the slightest sensation aggravates your nerves, try to move your work, study and other personal spaces as far away as you can from air vent currents, window treatments and any other obstacles that might inadvertently brush against your body.

3. If you enjoy the sensation of deep pressure, you might put light weights (store bought or some you have made yourself from sacks of small coins, pebbles, marbles, etc.) in the pockets of your jackets, sweaters and vests, even if this means you have to sew pockets in your clothing. Or you could get in the habit of carrying a heavy purse or backpack.

4. Find which kinds of fabric feel best on your skin and try to buy clothing, gloves, hats, towels, blankets, sheets, cooking mits and pot holders, scarves and so on, that are made from that material.

5. If washing your hair is a terrible issue for you, wear a very short hair cut that can be quickly washed in a few seconds. Do a dry shampoo by sprinkling corn starch or scent-free powder in your hair (if you can tolerate the tactile sensation of those textures) leaving it in for a few minutes, then brushing it out. Or consider wearing hats and scarves to cover your hair when it becomes unruly, but not quite desperate enough for a washing. Remember though, that you will have to wash your hair at least once a week or you risk getting lice, scalp ailments and social rejections.

6. If you need to stimulate the sensitive nerve endings around your mouth, do not chew pencils and pens which might break and splinter into your mouth, instead chew hard substances like paraffin wax, thick rubber tubing, gum or heavy plastic straws.

7. If you like to squish and scrunch things, fill balloons with flour, flour and rice, cornstarch, or some other pleasing substance, then squish away (only after the balloon has been tied shut with a knot); play with shaving cream before you use it; play with modeling clay; learn to bake bread the old fashioned way; garden; squeeze a small rubber ball; hold a small vibrating toy; or fiddle with a prepackaged bag of rice or beans. And do not worry if you need to do these things in public, they are easy to conceal. Just put them in small containers you can hide in your pockets or put them in your shoes to squish with your toes.

8. Use your personal hygiene routine as a sensory input center. Either very firmly or very lightly (depending on your preference) scrub your body with differently textured bath brushes and wash cloths until you find the combination of force and texture you enjoy.

Visual sensitivity

1. Wear sunglasses, visors or hats to protect yourself from the sun and overhead lights, but do not allow these to block or interfere with your vision.

2. Experiment with different colored light bulbs and different levels of bulb wattage to see which you like the best.

3. Surround yourself with colors that appeal to you.

4. If you are overwhelmed in large crowded areas, try putting your hands around your face and focus on things just in front of you, not those things in your peripheral vision. I often do this and have discovered that if I pretend to be rubbing my temples, as if I am warding off a headache, people do not react oddly when they see me.

5. Look down at the floor directly ahead of you, but only try this if you are with someone who can guide you around obstacles.

Auditory sensitivity

1. Wear earplugs designed for light sleepers, using caution to make sure you can still hear emergency vehicles, people when they are talking to you and any other sound that is important to your safety, learning and well-being. Avoid using cotton balls or facial tissues as earplugs, because they can create their own potentially disturbing frequency as air passes through the fibers of the cotton.

2. Simply try to avoid areas where different noises merge together, such as large sports stadiums, concert halls, busy malls, rooms filled with loud people and music, large cafeterias, etc. Consider earplugs if you do go to any of those places.

3. Wear stereo headphones to mask other noises, again making certain you can hear possibly important sounds.

4. Think about enrolling in an auditory integration training program.

Food sensitivity

1. If food presents a problem for you because of its texture, smell and/or taste, try to find at least a small handful of foods from each nutritional group you can accept and simply stick to eating those, even if it means you will bring your own food to restaurants and other people's homes.

2. Try dressing up mushy or slimy sensations by adding crunch foods like celery, nuts, seeds or carrots; anything you like that could bulk-up the soft texture.

3. Try eating the foods you really do not like, but think you need to eat for your health, when you are very relaxed and

when you can put your thoughts on something else like your favorite book or television show. Begin by eating just one or two tiny bites, working your way up to a full bite size only if you are able.

4. If you feel you can, experiment with new recipes that change the way your aversive food looks and tastes. For example, you might be able to eat a small portion of a banana, if it is mixed in a chocolate shake, or you might be able to eat some cauliflower if it is mashed with a potato.

5. Talk to your doctor to see if you should be taking supplements to fortify your restricted diet.

Olfactory sensitivity

1. Put a bit of your favorite smell, if you can find it in a liquid or paste, on the end of a cotton ball or on the inside of your arm, and smell it when other smells overwhelm you.

2. Wear nose plugs when you are in a private area.

3. Purchase only non-scented cleaning and bathing products.

4. Politely ask those around you to please not wear perfumes or eat heavy smelling foods in your presence.

5. Write your local political representative about the possibility of passing new laws which restrict or prohibit the use of advertisements that smell, such as perfume and cologne flyers or washer and dryer soap samples, that often come in magazines or to private mail boxes.

Thoughts for the Non-AS Support People

When my daughter was diagnosed with Asperger's Syndrome, her doctors gave me one outstanding piece of counsel. They told me that my husband and I would now become the experts on AS. We, in effect, would stand as her greatest advocates. The truth of their prophecy has been shown virtually every day. The general public is largely uneducated in AS. I have grown to believe that this is the single most damaging element to the AS cause, that is, understanding and acceptance. Without knowledge of the symptoms, outcomes and even confounding attributes, it is nearly impossible for others to recognize and support AS individuals. Education. This is the key, the very accessible key. International, national, regional, state and local Asperger support groups abound (see Appendix VII).

The WWW is a virtual AS classroom, brimming with dozens of sites devoted to AS research, personal stories, medical implications, educational and employment considerations. Even the mass media has begun to embrace the cause by showcasing AS families and persons. Slowly, the world of Asperger's Syndrome is finding its way to the mainstream mind. With your help, it will get there faster. If one thing is certain in the AS world, it is simply that the diagnosis means different things to different people at different times in their lives. Put another way, AS affects individuals in varying degrees and in varying ways. This reality can make it quite difficult to suggest a pat and foolproof summary of how others can lend effective support. Yet, because support from others is so often extremely instrumental to the complete well-being of an AS person, it seems imperative that something concrete be suggested, even if it serves as only a guideline and never as an absolute. The following guide is an attempt to do just that. It is directed toward anyone who considers themselves a source of support for AS individuals.

Family, spouse and close friends

- Realize the importance of your support, even if the AS person is unaware of it. You will, in many ways, serve as a role model for behavior, a counselor when feelings of confusion and insecurities mingle toward the surface, and a calming influence should things spring out of control.

- Try to find ways to deal with the stress you will face as the main support system. Take time outs, promise yourself opportunities to unwind and relax, seek a mentor or counselor of your own, should you feel it is called for.

- Expect to give only what you can, never taking too much away from your own identity. Try to reach a compromise between the needs of the AS person in your life and your own. For instance, you might relish socializing, while your AS friend might abhor it. You could work out an arrangement that finds you going places with other friends while your AS friend stays at home with a good book or a favorite movie you brought home for her to enjoy. One caveat, try never to make the AS person feel less important because they do not share parts of your identity.

- Understand people cannot snap out of AS traits, instantly leaving behind obsessive compulsive rituals or rigid thinking or literal mindedness. Realize it takes continuing education, behavioral modification training, time and personal experience memories to help people with AS find appropriately effective coping skills. Keep these realities in mind when you begin discussions, particularly heated debates or arguments with an AS person. If you employ logic, concrete and controlled language, specific examples and an objectively open mind, you will be far more likely to keep the channels of communication between you and your AS friend open and meaningful.

○ Help the AS person establish a small group of friends who are educated in AS and able and willing to accept the nuances and intricacies of the syndrome. Be confident that AS people normally enjoy friendships, they simply might be confused in knowing how to begin and maintain them.

○ Try to help the AS person avoid the kinds of pitfalls that will send them reeling with confusion and consequent dismay. Help them avoid situations that will tax their sensory sensitivities; encourage them to turn their hobbies and interests into both therapeutic and career opportunities; be prepared to help them organize their home lives by assisting them with any number of things such as shopping, housekeeping, child rearing practices, day-to-day chores and responsibilities, wardrobe selections, and society's expectations.

○ Find direct ways to reassure them of your affection and friendship. Share their hobbies, follow their interests, tell them you like listening to their stories, laugh at their jokes, go places with them, in short – enjoy them just like you enjoy other important people in your life.

○ Do not condescend or patronize. AS people are not stupid, they are not without wits. They simply view the world through different windows. Try to see the world as they do, and you will likely come away refreshed and renewed.

Educators

- Keep in mind that many AS people lack organizational skills, therefore do not be surprised when they forget assignment due dates, homework, classroom materials, etc. Be as flexible as you possibly can. Try to assist the student by giving him or her visual reminders such as a picture of all the things that should be brought to class each day, a calendar with assignment dates highlighted and marked in bold ink, and notes on brightly colored paper that serve as memos and reminders for the day, week or month. Establish a peer mentor who can be responsible for calling the AS student with reminders and hints on what to bring to class and how to prepare for assignments. And send important notes and dates home to family members who can also make reminder calls.

- Remember that people with AS have problems with abstract and conceptual thinking. Use very concrete examples and explanations, and literal and direct word meanings when you are explaining thoughts that involve high levels of problem solving skills. Suggest tutoring services, if you feel they are necessary, and be certain the student has taken all the prerequisite courses they need before they enter your class. Skipping courses simply to accommodate a class schedule is a terrible idea for the AS person. They need as much background building material as possible.

- Note that odd behaviors can often come as a result of stress. If you see your AS student becoming noticeably upset or engaging in self calming rituals, ask them in private if they might not like to take a few moments away from the classroom to relax or if they need a session with a guidance counselor.

- Be prepared to hear some different kinds of discussions and questions from your AS student. Realize they are not intentionally trying to goad you or act out rude behavior. Know that weak social skills and an honest misunderstanding of the language or logic you might be using could very likely be at the root of these kinds of situations.

○ Avoid idioms, words with double meanings, sarcasm and subtle humor.

○ Know the AS person probably has difficulty reading non-verbal messages. Do not rely solely on these to convey your messages.

○ Try to use plenty of visual aids, allow the student to use tape recorders, be flexible in peer assignment requirements and classroom presentation expectations.

○ Keep changes in routine and class structure to a minimum.

○ Help the student find a seat in the class that will keep visual and auditory distractions to a minimum.

Employers

○ Always keep in mind that what AS people might lack in terms of social skills or flexibility can be more than compensated for through their tremendous sense of loyalty, dedication, strong knowledge base and solid capabilities.

○ Guide the AS employee to a job that matches their interests knowing that this can be a very strong motivating factor which works to help the AS person make incredible strides and accomplishments in that very field.

○ Encourage jobs that require few social skills and little socializing. Capitalize on the fact that many AS people might reach success in areas that other persons would normally find too lonely or isolated.

- Assign freelance projects that can be completed at home where the AS person might feel far more comfortable and therefore far more able to really concentrate on doing an excellent job.

- Take advantage of a typical AS characteristic – a desire for routine and repetition. Help the AS person find jobs that follow a pattern and are predictable. This will do quite a lot to prevent stress and anxiety which could interfere with high productivity.

- Prepare the AS person in advance before making changes in job expectations or responsibilities, office relocations, schedule changes and staff shifts. Again, stress and anxiety will be reduced if change is kept to a minimum or, at least, gradually made.

- Use a mentoring system. Let an empathetic co-worker who has ideally been educated about AS assist the AS employee with such things as group projects, informal and formal presentations, following and understanding company rules and expectations, maintaining composure and professionalism in social situations (though contact with customers and clients should probably be kept to a minimum unless the AS person is well trained in how to handle themselves in such situations) and even in finding their way around the physical environment of the company.

- Ask the AS person what she or he needs in terms of environmental considerations. For example, specific lighting and acceptable noise level requirements.

Support Groups and Other Helpful Resources

Support groups and general information

Each of these groups is committed to Asperger's Syndrome and other related developmental disorders. Those on-line typically offer additional links for further study.

American Occupational Therapy Association, Inc.
4720 Montgomery Lane,
Bethesda, MD 20814-3425
Telephone: 1-301-652-2682.
Fax: 1-301-652-7711
http://www.aota.org/index.html

The ASPEN Society of America, Inc.
(Asperger Syndrome Education Network)
P.O. Box 2577
Jacksonville, FL 32203-2577
Telephone: 1-904-745-6741
http://www.asperger.org/

Asperger's Syndrome Support Network, associated with the Autistic Family Support Association, Victoria, Australia
Asperger's Syndrome Support Network
C/O VACCA
PO Box 235
Ashburton Victoria 3147
Australia
http://home.vicnet.net.au/~autism/assn/asperger.htm

The Autism Society of America
7910 Woodmont Ave, Suite 650,
Bethesda, MD 20814-3015
Telephone: 1-800-3-AUTISM

Fax: 1-301-657-0869
http://www.autism-society.org/asa_home.html

The National Autistic Society
393 City Road,
London EC1V 1NE
Telephone: 0171 833 2299
Registered charity no. 269425
Email: nas@mailbox.ulcc.ac.uk

O.A.S.I.S. (Online Asperger Syndrome Information and Support)
http://www.udel.edu/bkirby/asperger/

Sensory Integration International (SII)
The Ayres Clinic
Telephone 1-310-320-2335

Sensory Integration Resource Center
http://www.sinetwork.org/index.htm

Best books

These books are among those I routinely see recommended by parents, researchers and individuals with Asperger's Syndrome.

Asperger's Syndrome: A Guide for Parents and Professionals
Tony Attwood
Foreword by Lorna Wing
Jessica Kingsley Publishers, London, 1998.
ISBN 1 85302 577 1

This is the book that changed my life. One of the best layman's book on Asperger's Syndrome. A must-have not only for teachers and parents, but for anyone who is just learning to understand Asperger's Syndrome.

Asperger Syndrome: A Guide for Educators and Parents
Brenda Smith Myles and Richard L. Simpson
PRO-ED, Austin, Texas, 1998.
ISBN 0 89079 727 7

This book uses practical and easy to understand language to explore topics such as social enhancement, behavioral management, academic support and the impact AS has on families.

Autism and Asperger's Syndrome
Uta Frith, ed.

Cambridge, Cambridge University Press, 1991.
ISBN 0 521386 08X

This book is quite technical, but it is a very important book that does much to explain Asperger's research.

Higher Functioning Adolescents and Young Adults with Autism: A Teacher's Guide
Ann Fullerton, ed., Joyce Stratton, Phyllis Coyne, and Carol Gray
PRO-ED, Austin, Texas, 1996.
ISBN 0 890796 815

This insightful and helpful guide explores the issues facing adolescents and young adults, suggests how to adapt classroom materials and provides ideas for social skills training.

Sensory Integration and the Child
Jean Ayres
Western Psychological Services, Los Angeles, 1979.
ISBN 0 874241 588

A comprehensive and important resource for understanding and helping the person who experiences Sensory Integration dysfunction written by Jean Ayres, the founder of Sensory Integration therapy.

Teaching Your Child the Language of Social Success
Marshall P. Duke, Stephen Nowicki, and Elisabeth A. Martin
Peachtree Publishers, LTD, Atlanta, Georgia, 1996.
ISBN 1 56145 126 6

A complete book filled with many useful and clear ideas for helping people, not just children, understand and use nonverbal communication and related language processes.

The Out-of-Sync Child: Recognizing and Coping with Sensory Integration Dysfunction
Carol Stock Kranowitz, Foreword by Larry B. Silver
Perigee, 1998.
ISBN 0 39952 386 3

Though this book is not written solely for the person with Asperger's Syndrome, it does contain information and suggestions about Sensory Integration Dysfunction that will apply to anyone facing those difficulties.

Thinking in Pictures and Other Reports of my Life with Autism
Temple Grandin

Doubleday, New York, 1995.
ISBN 0 67977 289 8

A very personal account of what autism is and what it is like to be affected by it.

Publishing companies and bookstores that offer Asperger's Syndrome titles

Jessica Kingsley Publishers

In the UK:
116 Pentonville Road
London N1 9JB
England
Tel: +44 (0)171 833 2307
Fax: +44 (0)171 837 2917

In the US:
325 Chestnut Street
Philadelphia, PA 19106
USA
Tel: (toll free) 1 800 821 8312
Tel: 1 215 625 8900
Fax: 1 215 625 2940
http://www.jkp.com

Future Horizons

720 N. Fielder Arlington, TX 76012
Tel: 1 800 489 0727
http://www.futurehorizons-autism.com/

Learning Disabilities Association

4156 Library Road
Pittsburgh, PA 15234

PRO-ED

8700 Shoal Creek Blvd
Austin, TX 78757
Tel: (toll free) 1-800 897 3202
Tel: 1-512 451 3246
Fax: 1-512 451 8542
http://www.proedinc.com/

Glossary

Auditory Discrimination: The brain's ability to separate important sounds (speaking voices) from extraneous sounds (traffic noise); locate where sounds are coming from (the front of the classroom or the rear of the classroom); maintain focus on essential tasks (studying) while ignoring outside noises that might interfere with concentration (music in the background). An inability to discriminate between sounds typically results in weak study skills.

Auditory Sensitivity: A disorder that interferes with an individual's ability to analyze or make sense of sound information taken in through the ears. Persons affected by auditory sensitivity can find certain noises and sounds frightening, painful, distorted, confusing, and overwhelming to the point where everyday activities are impossible to enjoy and/or engage in.

Bilateral Coordination: The body's ability to use its two sides cohesively and in coordination. Without bilateral coordination, a person is likely to experience difficulties in both fine motor movement activities such as using eating utensils, dressing or writing; and gross motor movement activities such as running, throwing, dancing or skipping. Poor reading skills are also often correlated with inadequate bilateral coordination.

Echolalia: A uniquely proficient and often remarkably sophisticated ability to parrot or mimic someone else's voice, speaking pattern, words and/or mannerisms.

Obsessive Compulsive Disorder: A confused perception of reality which causes an individual to obsess on a perceived worry or thought (is the iron turned off, is the door locked. There are too many germs on this doorknob, etc.) that causes great anxiety and concern. The anxieties and concerns are only elevated for the person if they perform certain compulsive activities or mental acts (checking and rechecking a dozen times to be certain the iron is off and the door locked, or repetitive hand washing for sixty minutes, counting to ten over and over again, for example). In order for these patterns to be a true disorder, they must occur frequently enough to interfere with normal daily living and routines.

Olfactory Sensitivity: A disorder that interferes with an individual's ability to cope with the sense of smell. Persons affected by olfactory sensitivity can find certain smells stressful, physically sickening, and completely repulsing. This can often make it difficult, if not impossible for the person to eat certain foods and/or concentrate in certain environments.

Pedantic Speech: Overly formal speech characterized by limited and literal interpretations of words.

Prosody: The vocal tone and qualities of speech. The 'it's not what you said, but how you said it' characteristics of spoken language that often leave people with Asperger's Syndrome unable to accurately discern the meaning behind other individuals' words, and unable to adequately express their own intended thoughts.

Sensory Integration: The process by which the brain organizes sensory input so one can interact with one's environment effectively and meaningfully.

Sensory Integration Dysfunction: A marked inability to properly integrate sensory input, usually as a result of a neurological disorder or irregularity. Persons who experience sensory integration dysfunction often experience anxiety attacks, headaches, disorientation, confusion and problems in learning.

Spatial relation: A visual processing disorder that makes it difficult to position and coordinate objects in space.

Stim: A self-stimulating behavior (flapping hands, licking, spinning, rocking, etc.) designed to calm or de-stress.

Tactile Sensitivity: A condition that occurs when nerves under the surface of the skin miscommunicate information to the brain. As a result, an individual either overreacts or underreacts to any number of sensations including light and firm pressure, pain and temperature. A dysfunction in this ability can lead to an aversion to certain types of textures (wet, rough, sandy, slick, slimy, etc.) and certain behaviors (hair washing, hand shaking, craft making, pencil holding, etc.). Dysfunction can also expose an individual to stress, irritability, distractibility, and a desire for isolation.

Ticking: An involuntary set of small or large muscle movements or vocal utterances that result in a habitual and uncontrollable action such as blinking, teeth clicking, nose scrunching, coughing, grunting, etc. Ticking often causes anxiety, embarrassment and feelings of shame in the individual affected. Should the individual try too hard to control the action, they will likely face nervous tension and an inability to concentrate on other matters.

Visual Sensitivity: A visual processing disorder that weakens an individual's ability to understand, interpret and process information gathered through the eyes. This can result in poor reading and writing skills, an inability to judge objects in space in relation to one another properly and disorientation in following directions and finding one's way.

References

Attwood, T. (1998) *Asperger's Syndrome: A Guide for Parents and Professionals.* London: Jessica Kingsley Publishers.

Frith, U. (ed) (1991) *Autism and Asperger Syndrome.* Cambridge: Cambridge University Press.

Gillberg, C. and Gillberg, C. (1989) 'Asperger Syndrome – Some epidemiological considerations: A research note.' *Journal of Child Psychology and Psychiatry 30,* 631–638.

Rimland, B. (1990) 'Sound sensitivity in autism.' *Autism Research Review International 4, 1 and 6.*

Wing, L. and Attwood, A. (1987) 'Syndromes of autism and atypical development.' In D. Cohen and A. Donnellan (eds) *Handbook of Autism and Pervasive Developmental Disorders.* New York: John Wiley and Sons.

Wing, L. (1981) 'Asperger's Syndrome: A clinical account.' *Psychological Medicine 11,* 115–130.